Celebrate Chicago!
A Taste of Our Town

YOU'RE INVITED
City Lights
Cocktail Party
DATE
June 2
TIME
8:00 p.m.
PLACE
1447 North Astor
RSVP
Regrets Only

A Cookbook from the
Junior League of Chicago

Celebrate Chicago!

A Taste of Our Town

A Cookbook from the
Junior League of Chicago

A TASTE OF OUR TOWN

Chicago's skyline

Additional copies of *Celebrate Chicago! A Taste of Our Town*
may be obtained by writing or calling:
Celebrate Chicago! A Taste of Our Town
The Junior League of Chicago, Inc.
1447 North Astor Street
Chicago, Illinois 60610
(312) 664-4462

Please enclose your return address with a check payable to
Celebrate Chicago! in the amount of $21.95 per book plus $4.00
shipping and handling. Illinois residents add $1.92 sales tax per book.

First Edition

Library of Congress Catalogue Number 96-077930
ISBN 0-9611622-3-6

Edited, Designed and Manufactured by Favorite Recipes® Press
P.O. Box 305142, Nashville, Tennessee 37230
1-800-358-0560
Book Design: Steve Newman

The Junior League of Chicago, Inc. is a not-for-profit organization
whose purpose is exclusively educational and charitable.
The proceeds realized from the sale of *Celebrate Chicago! A Taste of Our Town*
will be used for projects The Junior League of Chicago, Inc.
supports in the Chicago community.

A TASTE OF OUR TOWN

Mission Statement

The Junior League of Chicago, Inc. is a metropolitan organization of women committed to promoting voluntarism, developing the potential of women and improving the community through effective action and leadership of trained volunteers. The Junior League of Chicago, Inc. reaches out to women of all races, religions and national origins who demonstrate an interest in and a commitment to voluntarism. Its purpose is exclusively educational and charitable.

Founded in 1912, the Junior League of Chicago, Inc. provides a positive force for change within the communities it serves. The League develops projects in response to a community need, independently or in cooperation with a community agency. The projects share a common focus of "Strengthening Today's Family." The Junior League of Chicago, Inc. currently has three core program areas to meet specific needs of today's family: Children at Risk, Education and Homelessness. Each year approximately 2,000 members contribute over 200,000 hours of volunteer service to the community.

JUNIOR LEAGUE OF CHICAGO

2,000 Women Making a Difference

A TASTE OF OUR TOWN

Contents

Buckingham Fountain is the centerpiece of Chicago's Grant Park.

Acknowledgements

Junior League Committee Members

Mimi Sardou Ogden (1995–97)   Kim Suhrheinrich Hartman (96–97)   Mary Lois Faulhaber (95–96)

Recipe Collection:	Grace Everett	Recipe Testing:	Julie Pfeiffer Brooks, Kim S. Hartman
Layout & Design:	Sharon R. Knitter	Copy & Content:	Diana Sweemer
Marketing:	Kristin A. Merrigan	Public Relations:	Kimberly Blazek Dahlborn
Business Manager:	Karen M. Graham		

Liz Asbjornson, Polly Bauer, Amy Bomm, Stephanie Bournakis, Bridget Bulger, Ann Cain, Kelly J. Carafotes, Cynthia Halverson Chase, Heather Coleman, Melissa M. Cutting, Elizabeth Daliere, Abbie Deneen, Heather Tatham Dubinsky, Carrie Eggerichs, Lori Fewster, Lee Ellen Fox, Susan Fraser, Laurel E. Gilbert, Elizabeth Goebel, Sue-Gray Goller, Ann M. Gowan, Mary Gresge, Chris Gretchko, Cynthia A. Humphrey, Betsy Johnston, Christine A. Junker, Kristin Kjelstrom, Elizabeth Kennedy Knight, Sallie Lycette, Kristin A. Magnuson, Kathy Malherbe, Elizabeth Marchetta, Gail Quigley McCarthy, Kathi M. Mettler, Laura A. Moran, Clara Nelson, Kitty Knox Oldham, Laura J. Pasek, Cathryn L. Ploger, Suzanne Smart Pollack, Stephanie L. Powell, Kate K. Prange, Linda Reynolds, Jennifer Rowe, Mary Rownd, Deborah Schmidt, Deena E. Schencker, Anne Smith, Susan Smith, Judy Goodwin Trunsky, Anne Tucker, Ann Turnbull, Karen Walsh, Caitlin Nammack Weissman, and Barbara Ann Wright

Special thanks to:

The Junior League of Chicago Board of Directors, Kim Beard, Kim Bolden, Janet Buckstein, Julie Drewniak, Carrie Eggerichs, Elizabeth Hurley, Suellen Johnson, Julie Rogers, Liz Sharp, and Robyn Menna Strausser

Credits:

Food Photography	Sharon Hoogstraten
Food Stylist	Lenni Gilbert
Neighborhood Photography	See page 240
Original Cover Art and Illustrations	Caitlin Nammack
Art Direction	Lisa Schumacher
Props	Jim Brust, Robert Adrian
	Rick Bayless, Frontera Grill/Topolobampo
Flowers	Rick Koebler, Scarborough Faire

A TASTE OF OUR TOWN

Introduction

Celebrate Chicago! A Taste of Our Town. The Chicago most people see is the commercial and cultural heart of the city. Whether it be the impressive skyline, the world-famous architecture, the shopping or the many events the city offers, Chicago's core strengths are manifest. However, much is to be found in the enclaves that make up Chicago's neighborhoods, each with its own unique character, history and influence.

This collection of recipes reflects Chicago's rich diversity and heritage. While there are forty landmark districts within the city limits alone, we have chosen to focus on ten neighborhoods which significantly enrich the lives of Chicagoans, as well as those who only pass through. Discover the history behind Bridgeport, the neighborhood which housed the Chicago stockyards, or take a trip through the Gold Coast, home to the Junior League of Chicago. Whichever route you take, you will discover there is much more to the city than you imagined.

Recipes were collected from league members, families and friends, restaurants, and some of Chicago's celebrities. Using the freshest ingredients, they vary from simple and elegant to extravagant. Whether planning an outdoor barbecue with a couple of friends or a special occasion dinner, you are sure to find several menu ideas from which to choose.

While recipes are the main focus of any cookbook, this collection also serves as a tribute to the great political and human entity that make Chicago the foremost city of the Midwest. Explore Chicago's neighborhoods and their treasures while sampling some of the finest cuisine the city has to offer. Enjoy!

NEIGHBO

Gold Coast

The wealthiest of Chicago helped rebuild the city after the great Chicago Fire in 1871; they financed and developed the Magnificent Mile and took up residence in the Gold Coast. Thus, the name evolved from the residents of that time. Many of Chicago's great architects, including Daniel Burnham and Louis Sullivan, began to leave their mark on the city after the fire. While new iron and steel buildings were being constructed in the Loop in the architectural style of the Chicago School, graceful mansions were dotting North Lake Shore Drive and its neighboring streets. Many of them are still standing today, including the Junior League of Chicago headquarters on Astor Street, built in 1900.

Once the playground for the carriage trade, the Gold Coast's Magnificent Mile, stretching between the Chicago River and Oak Street, is now one of the world's most exclusive shopping areas. The John Hancock Building on Michigan Avenue is its most prominent landmark. Built in 1969, this one-hundred-story tower rises more than one thousand feet.

The Gold Coast remains one of Chicago's most affluent neighborhoods. Its diverse residents live, work and play within this beautiful lakefront neighborhood.

Rowhouses on Astor Street

City Lights Cocktail Party

Polenta Stars 21

Asparagus Cheese Puffs 15

Prosciutto and Bleu Cheese Pears 22

Brie Wheel 26

Smoked Salmon and Goat Cheese 26

Hotel Ritz Champagne 32

STARTERS & BEVERAGES

Polenta Stars

Starters & Beverages

Asparagus Cheese Puffs, 15

Melitzanosalta
   (Eggplant Dip), 16

Tzatziki, 16

Black Bean Salsa, 17

Black Bean Roll-Ups, 17

Bruschetta, 18

Crostini with Topping, 18

Pepper Biscuits with
   Cheddar-Pecan
   Spread, 19

Stuffed French Bread, 20

Pesto and Brie Canapés, 20

Polenta Stars, 21

Pickled Radishes, 21

Prosciutto and Bleu
   Cheese Pears, 22

Jamaican Jerk Chicken, 22

Chicken Verona Crepes, 23

Curried Lamb in Cucumber
   Cornucopias, 24

Smoked Salmon and Goat
   Cheese, 26

Brie Wheel, 26

Basil Cheese Strata, 27

Pesto Cheesecake, 28

Tuna Pâté, 29

Marinated Onions, 29

Mustard Chicken Pâté with
   Ham and Olives, 30

Authentic Guacamole, 30

Michael Jordan's Portobello
   Mushrooms, 31

Shrimp and Avocado
   Quesadillas, 32

Hotel Ritz Champagne, 32

Champage Punch, 33

Crimson Royale, 33

Daiquiri Punch, 34

Eskimo Latté, 34

Lime Zest Cooler, 35

Margaritas, 35

Asparagus Cheese Puffs

$^1/_2$ cup milk
$^1/_4$ cup water
3 tablespoons unsalted butter
$^3/_4$ teaspoon salt
$^1/_4$ teaspoon cayenne
$^1/_4$ teaspoon coriander

$^3/_4$ cup flour
3 eggs
4 ounces asparagus, trimmed
$^1/_2$ cup coarsely grated
Gruyère cheese
$^1/_4$ cup grated Parmesan cheese

Butter 2 baking sheets lightly. Line with parchment paper and butter paper.

Bring milk, water, butter, salt, cayenne and coriander to a boil in saucepan; reduce heat to medium-low. Add flour.

Beat with wooden spoon for 1 minute or until dough pulls from bottom and side of saucepan.

Cool for 4 minutes. Transfer dough to food processor container. Pulse 5 to 6 times. Add eggs 1 at a time, processing well after each addition; dough will be smooth and shiny. Cool slightly.

Blanch asparagus in a small amount of water in saucepan for 1 to 2 minutes. Drain and rinse under cold water; chop coarsely.

Combine asparagus, Gruyère cheese and Parmesan cheese with dough in food processor container and mix well. Drop by rounded teaspoonfuls 1 inch apart onto prepared baking sheets. Smooth tops with moistened pastry brush.

Place on middle oven rack. Bake at 400 degrees for 25 minutes. Transfer to a serving platter.

May prepare in advance and reheat in 350-degree oven.

Yield: 48 servings

Melitzanosalta (Eggplant Dip)

1 eggplant
¹/₃ cup chopped green olives
¹/₄ cup mayonnaise
3 tablespoons lemon juice
2 tablespoons grated onion
2 tablespoons minced fresh parsley
1 tablespoon olive oil
1 clove of garlic, minced
Salt and pepper to taste
Minced fresh parsley
Kalamata olives

Pierce eggplant in several places with fork. Place on baking sheet.

Bake at 400 degrees for 45 minutes. Split eggplant. Let stand until cool.

Scoop eggplant pulp into blender or food processor container. Add green olives, mayonnaise, lemon juice, onion, 2 tablespoons minced parsley, olive oil and garlic.

Process until puréed. Season with salt and pepper. Chill, covered, for 2 hours or longer.

Spoon into a serving bowl. Top with minced fresh parsley and kalamata olives. Serve with assorted party breads.

Yield: 10 to 12 servings

Tzatziki

2 cups plain yogurt
1 small cucumber, peeled, seeded, coarsely ground
2 cloves of garlic, crushed
1 tablespoon fresh lemon juice
1 teaspoon grated onion
1 teaspoon olive oil
1 teaspoon chopped fresh dillweed, or ¹/₂ teaspoon dried dillweed
Salt and freshly ground pepper to taste

Drain yogurt and cucumber in separate cheesecloth-lined colanders.

Combine yogurt, cucumber, garlic, lemon juice, onion, olive oil, dillweed, salt and pepper in bowl and mix well.

Serve as dip with fresh vegetables or as sandwich sauce for gyros.

Yield: 16 servings

Black Bean Salsa

2 (15-ounce) cans black beans, drained, rinsed
1 (16-ounce) can whole kernel corn, drained
1 red bell pepper, chopped
$^1/_2$ cup chopped fresh cilantro
$^1/_2$ cup chopped green onions
Juice of 2 large limes
1 tablespoon cumin
Garlic salt to taste
Tortilla chips

Combine beans, corn, red pepper, cilantro, green onions, lime juice, cumin and garlic salt in bowl and mix well.

Spoon into serving bowl. Serve with tortilla chips.

Yield: 4 cups

Black Bean Roll-Ups

1 (15-ounce) can black beans, drained
8 ounces cream cheese, softened
$^1/_4$ cup chopped fresh cilantro
5 to 7 green onions, chopped
1 medium red bell pepper, chopped
1 teaspoon ground red pepper
1 teaspoon cumin
1 teaspoon chili powder
1 teaspoon Tabasco sauce or hot pepper sauce
$^1/_2$ teaspoon garlic powder
$^1/_4$ teaspoon salt
Juice of $^1/_2$ lime
6 large flour tortillas

Combine beans, cream cheese, cilantro, green onions, bell pepper, red pepper, cumin, chili powder, Tabasco sauce, garlic powder and salt in bowl and mix well. Stir in lime juice until of the desired consistency; mixture should be thick but easy to spread.

Spread 2 to 3 tablespoons over entire surface of each tortilla; roll to enclose filling. Wrap tortillas in plastic wrap.

Chill for 6 to 12 hours. Cut each roll diagonally into 1-inch slices. Arrange cut side up on serving platter. Serve with salsa if desired.

Yield: 60 servings

Bruschetta

1 large bunch arugula or basil, trimmed,
finely chopped
8 ounces smoked mozzarella cheese,
finely chopped
2 tomatoes, seeded, finely chopped
Salt and pepper to taste
1 1/2 loaves Italian bread
2 cloves of garlic, cut into halves
1/4 cup extra-virgin olive oil

Combine arugula, cheese, tomatoes, salt and
pepper in bowl and mix well.

Cut bread diagonally into twelve 1/2-inch slices.
Place on baking sheet.

Broil 4 inches from heat source until brown,
turning once. Rub 1 side of each slice with garlic and
brush with 1/2 of the olive oil. Spread with arugula
mixture. Drizzle with remaining olive oil.

Arrange bruschetta on serving platter.

Yield: 12 servings

Crostini with Topping

Extra-virgin olive oil
1 loaf Italian bread, sliced
2 ripe pears, peeled, cut into quarters
Juice of 1/2 lemon
8 ounces Stilton cheese
2 tablespoons olive oil
2 tablespoons brandy
Pepper to taste

Brush baking sheet with extra-virgin olive oil.
Brush both sides of bread slices lightly with extra-
virgin olive oil. Arrange in single layer on prepared
baking sheet.

Bake at 375 degrees for 10 minutes, turning once.

Cut pear quarters lengthwise into halves. Cut 1/8
inch lengthwise through each slice, leaving end
intact. Fan slices on buttered baking sheet; drizzle
with lemon juice.

Broil for 6 to 10 minutes or until light brown. Let
stand until cool.

Beat cheese, 2 tablespoons olive oil and brandy in
bowl until creamy. Season with pepper. Spread on
crostini. Place on baking sheet.

Broil for 1 to 2 minutes or until bubbly. Top with
pear slices. Serve immediately.

May substitute grilled vegetables, thick salsa or
puréed seasoned white beans for pears. Use Italian
bread for hearty toppings and French bread for
spreads or lighter toppings.

Yield: 24 servings

Pepper Biscuits with Cheddar-Pecan Spread

4 ounces cream cheese, softened
$^1/_2$ cup sour cream
2 cups shredded sharp Cheddar cheese
$^1/_2$ cup finely chopped pecans
2 medium scallion bulbs, finely chopped
$^1/_4$ teaspoon salt
$^1/_4$ teaspoon freshly ground pepper
$^1/_4$ teaspoon hot pepper sauce
2 cups flour

1 tablespoon plus $^1/_4$ teaspoon baking powder
1 teaspoon sugar
$^1/_4$ teaspoon baking soda
$^1/_4$ teaspoon salt
2 teaspoons freshly ground pepper
3 tablespoons finely chopped fresh chives
6 tablespoons unsalted butter, chilled
1 cup buttermilk

Process cream cheese and sour cream in food processor until blended. Add Cheddar cheese. Pulse until smooth. Add pecans and scallions.

Pulse until combined. Add salt, pepper and hot pepper sauce. Pulse until mixed. May store, covered, in refrigerator for up to 3 days. Serve at room temperature.

Add crab meat or marinated shrimp for variety.

Combine flour, baking powder, sugar, baking soda, salt, pepper and 1 tablespoon of the chives in bowl and mix well. Cut in butter until crumbly. Add buttermilk, stirring until soft dough forms; do not overmix.

Knead lightly on floured surface until smooth. Roll $^1/_4$-inch thick; cut with $1^1/_2$-inch biscuit cutter or champagne glass. Arrange on baking sheet.

Bake at 425 degrees for 10 minutes or until golden brown. Let stand until cool. May freeze for future use and reheat in 350-degree oven.

Cut biscuits horizontally into halves. Spread each bottom half with 1 rounded teaspoon of the cheese mixture; top with remaining halves. Arrange on a serving platter. Sprinkle with remaining chopped chives.

Yield: 48 servings

Stuffed French Bread

1 loaf sourdough bread
1 cup butter, softened
$3/4$ cup finely chopped watercress
2 tablespoons Italian bread crumbs
16 ounces cream cheese, softened
$1/2$ to 1 tube anchovy paste
2 tablespoons capers
2 tablespoons chili powder
2 tablespoons finely chopped onion
1 tablespoon Worcestershire sauce
$1^{1}/2$ teaspoons Tabasco sauce
2 to 3 tablespoons caper liquid
Sprigs of watercress

Cut bread loaf lengthwise into halves. Remove center carefully, leaving 2-inch shell; discard center.

Combine butter, $3/4$ cup watercress and bread crumbs in bowl, beating until mixed.

Beat cream cheese in mixer bowl until creamy. Add enough anchovy paste to tint cream cheese beige, beating until blended. Stir in capers, chili powder, onion, Worcestershire sauce and Tabasco sauce. Add caper liquid, stirring until spreading consistency. Spoon cream cheese mixture into bottom half of loaf. Spoon butter mixture into top half of loaf. Press halves together; wrap in foil.

Chill for 4 to 6 hours. Cut chilled loaf into $1/8$-inch slices. Arrange on serving platter. Top with watercress sprigs.

Yield: 24 servings

Pesto and Brie Canapés

$1/2$ cup pine nuts
8 oil-pack sun-dried tomato halves, drained, finely chopped
2 small cloves of garlic, minced
$1/2$ cup freshly grated Parmesan cheese
$1/4$ cup olive oil
$1/3$ cup minced Italian parsley
1 tablespoon minced fresh basil
Freshly ground pepper
1 pound Brie cheese, rind removed, softened
1 baguette, cut diagonally into $1/4$-inch slices

Spread pine nuts on baking sheet. Toast at 350 degrees for 8 minutes or until golden brown, shaking baking sheet occasionally. Chop pine nuts coarsely.

Combine sun-dried tomatoes, garlic, Parmesan cheese, olive oil, parsley, basil and pepper in bowl and mix well. Beat Brie cheese in medium bowl until smooth.

Spread 1 rounded teaspoon Brie cheese on each baguette slice; top with $1/2$ teaspoon pesto. Sprinkle with pine nuts.

Arrange canapés on serving platter.

Yield: 48 servings

Polenta Stars

1 package instant polenta
Olive oil
4 ounces goat cheese
1 tablespoon chopped fresh dillweed
1 tablespoon olive oil
1 tablespoon dry white wine
8 oil-pack sun-dried tomatoes, drained, chopped
Sprigs of dillweed

Prepare polenta using package directions. Spread in 10x13-inch pan. Let stand until cool. Cut into shapes with a star cookie cutter or cookie cutter of your choice.

Fry polenta stars in olive oil in sauté pan until light brown on both sides. Drain on paper towel.

Mash goat cheese with fork in bowl. Stir in 1 tablespoon dillweed, 1 tablespoon olive oil, wine and 1/2 of the sun-dried tomatoes.

Spread cheese mixture on polenta stars; top with remaining sun-dried tomatoes. Arrange on a serving platter. Top with sprigs of dillweed.

Yield: 12 servings

Pickled Radishes

1 large bunch radishes, stems and tips removed
4 cups water
1 cup vinegar
1 tablespoon sugar
1 tablespoon salt
1 hot banana pepper, seeded, chopped
3 large fresh cloves of garlic, chopped
4 (1/2-inch) pieces of gingerroot, julienned

Place radishes in large glass jar.

Heat water, vinegar, sugar and salt in saucepan until hot. Add pepper, garlic and gingerroot and mix well. Pour over radishes.

Weight radishes down with glass filled with water. Chill, covered, for 6 to 10 hours. Drain and serve.

The radishes turn light pink and have a hot spicy flavor. Serve with assorted pâtés and assorted cheeses.

Yield: 4 to 6 servings

STARTERS & BEVERAGES

Prosciutto and Bleu Cheese Pears

1 large pear, cut into 12 wedges
1 cup water
1 to 2 tablespoons lemon juice
3 to 4 ounces thinly sliced prosciutto
$^1/_2$ cup crumbled bleu cheese
2 tablespoons cream cheese, softened
2 teaspoons milk

Dip pear wedges in mixture of water and lemon juice.

Cut prosciutto lengthwise into twelve 1$^1/_2$x6-inch strips.

Combine bleu cheese, cream cheese and milk in bowl, mixing until blended.

Spread 1 rounded teaspoon of cheese mixture on each prosciutto strip. Wrap each strip around a pear wedge.

Arrange seam side down on a serving platter. Chill, covered, for up to 2 hours.

Yield: 12 servings

Jamaican Jerk Chicken

4 boneless, skinless chicken breasts
3 bunches scallions, chopped
1 piece unpeeled gingerroot, chopped
$^3/_4$ cup soy sauce
1 teaspoon pepper sauce
1 teaspoon white pepper

Rinse chicken and pat dry; cut into small pieces. Place in shallow glass dish.

Combine scallions, gingerroot, soy sauce, pepper sauce and white pepper in blender container.

Process at high speed until blended. Pour over chicken, turning to coat.

Marinate, covered, in refrigerator for 1 to 10 hours, turning occasionally. Drain, reserving marinade.

Soak wooden skewers in water in bowl. Thread chicken on skewers. Place on rack in broiler pan; drizzle with some of reserved marinade.

Broil at 500 degrees for 10 minutes or until chicken is cooked through, turning occasionally.

Add additional pepper sauce for spicier chicken.

Yield: 8 to 10 servings

Chicken Verona Crepes

2 tablespoons butter	1 cup sliced green grapes
2 tablespoons flour	2 tablespoons chopped fresh parsley
1$^{1}/_{4}$ cups milk	$^{1}/_{2}$ cup sour cream
3 tablespoons dry sherry	$^{1}/_{2}$ cup sliced almonds, toasted
$^{1}/_{2}$ cup shredded Cheddar cheese	6 to 10 (7-inch) crepes
1 teaspoon instant chicken bouillon	$^{1}/_{2}$ cup sour cream
$^{1}/_{2}$ teaspoon salt	6 tablespoons chopped
2 cups chopped cooked chicken	fresh parsley

Heat butter in 2-quart saucepan over medium heat until melted. Stir in flour.
Cook for 1 minute, stirring constantly. Whisk in milk and sherry gradually, stirring constantly. Cook for 5 minutes or until thickened, stirring constantly. Stir in cheese, bouillon and salt. Cook for 2 minutes, stirring constantly. Add chicken and mix well.
Cook just until heated through, stirring constantly. Stir in grapes and 2 tablespoons parsley. Cook until heated through.
Add $^{1}/_{2}$ cup sour cream and blend well. Remove from heat. Stir in almonds.
Place crepes on lightly buttered baking sheet. Spoon $^{1}/_{2}$ cup hot chicken mixture onto center of each crepe; fold over sides to enclose filling.
Bake at 375 degrees for 10 minutes or until edges begin to curl.
Top with $^{1}/_{2}$ cup sour cream and 6 tablespoons parsley.

Yield: 6 to 10 servings

Curried Lamb in Cucumber Cornucopias

1 (1-pound) seedless cucumber
1 medium onion, finely chopped
6 ounces lean ground leg of lamb
2 tablespoons currants
2¹/₄ teaspoons curry powder
¹/₂ teaspoon salt

¹/₄ teaspoon cinnamon
¹/₈ teaspoon freshly ground pepper
1¹/₂ teaspoons chopped fresh mint
1 tablespoon plus 2 teaspoons plain
low-fat yogurt
36 fresh mint leaves

Cut cucumber widthwise into 3¹/₂-inch-long sections. Slice sections lengthwise with vegetable peeler or mandoline into flat rectangular slices; discard seeds.

Sauté onion in nonstick skillet sprayed with nonstick cooking spray for 10 to 15 minutes or until tender. Stir in lamb, currants, curry powder, salt, cinnamon and pepper.

Cook over medium-high heat for 10 to 20 minutes or until lamb is brown and cooked through, stirring frequently. Remove from heat. Stir in chopped mint and yogurt.

Shape 1 of the cucumber slices into a cone shape. Fill with 1 to 1¹/₂ teaspoons of the lamb mixture. Top with a mint leaf. Arrange on a serving platter.

Repeat process with remaining cucumber slices and remaining lamb mixture. Serve immediately.

Yield: 36 servings

Vintage walkups and high-rise condominiums on Chicago's Gold Coast

Smoked Salmon and Goat Cheese

5 ounces goat cheese
$^1/_4$ cup plain yogurt
3 small heads Belgian endive, separated
into spears
4 ounces smoked salmon, thinly sliced,
cut into thin strips
Juice of 1 lemon
2 tablespoons chopped fresh dillweed
Freshly ground pepper to taste

Combine goat cheese and yogurt in bowl, mixing until blended.

Spread 1 teaspoon of the cheese mixture on each endive spear. Top with salmon strip. Arrange on serving platter.

Drizzle with lemon juice and sprinkle with dillweed and pepper just before serving.

Yield: 30 to 40 servings

Brie Wheel

1 (5-pound) round Brie cheese with rind
1 cup golden currants
1 cup finely chopped pecans
1 cup chopped fresh dillweed
$^3/_4$ cup multicolored peppercorns
1 cup almond halves, toasted

Remove rind from top of the Brie cheese. Score into 10 sections.

Sprinkle currants, pecans, dillweed, peppercorns and almonds alternately in the 10 sections, pressing gently.

Chill, covered, in the refrigerator. Let stand at room temperature for 30 minutes before serving.

Flavor is enhanced if chilled for 4 to 10 hours.

Yield: 40 servings

Basil Cheese Strata

8 ounces cream cheese, softened
4 ounces blue-veined cheese or
goat cheese, softened
1 cup loosely packed basil leaves
$^3/_4$ cup fresh spinach
$^1/_4$ cup fresh Italian parsley
1 teaspoon minced garlic

$^1/_4$ cup olive oil
$^1/_4$ cup finely chopped walnuts
1 cup freshly grated
Parmesan cheese
$^1/_4$ cup slivered sun-dried
tomatoes, patted dry

Line 2x5-inch loaf pan with plastic wrap, allowing overhang at sides.

Mix cream cheese and blue-veined cheese in medium bowl; set aside.

Combine basil leaves, spinach, parsley and garlic in food processor container.

Add olive oil in a stream with food processor running, processing until smooth. Pour into large bowl.

Add walnuts and Parmesan cheese and mix well.

Layer $^1/_3$ of the cream cheese mixture, half the spinach mixture, half the tomatoes, half the remaining cream cheese mixture, remaining spinach mixture, remaining tomatoes and remaining cream cheese mixture in prepared loaf pan. Cover with overhanging plastic wrap. Chill for 12 to 24 hours.

Let stand for 20 minutes to soften before serving. Invert onto platter and remove plastic wrap.

Serve with hearty crackers or thinly sliced French bread.

Yield: 10 to 12 servings

Pesto Cheesecake

1 tablespoon butter, softened
$1/4$ cup fine dried Italian
bread crumbs
2 tablespoons freshly grated
Parmesan cheese
16 ounces cream cheese, softened
1 cup ricotta cheese
$1/2$ cup freshly grated
Parmesan cheese

$1/4$ teaspoon salt
$1/8$ teaspoon cayenne
3 eggs
$1/2$ cup pesto
$1/4$ cup pine nuts
Sprigs of basil

Spread butter over bottom and side of springform pan. Sprinkle with mixture of bread crumbs and 2 tablespoons Parmesan cheese.

Beat cream cheese, ricotta cheese, $1/2$ cup Parmesan cheese, salt and cayenne in mixer bowl until light and fluffy. Add eggs 1 at a time, beating well after each addition. Spoon $1/2$ of the mixture into another bowl. Add pesto to remaining half and mix well.

Spoon pesto mixture into prepared pan; smooth top. Spread cheese mixture evenly over top; sprinkle with pine nuts.

Bake at 375 degrees for 45 minutes or until set. Cool on wire rack. Chill, tightly covered with plastic wrap, for 8 to 10 hours.

Run knife around side of pan; remove side. Transfer to serving platter. Top with basil. Garnish with 2 fanned strawberries. May surround cheesecake with strawberries and grapes. Serve with wheat crackers.

Yield: 18 servings

Tuna Pâté

1 (7-ounce) can water-pack tuna, drained
3 ounces cream cheese, softened
1 tablespoon mayonnaise
1 (4-ounce) jar capers, drained
1 tablespoon horseradish
$^1/_2$ teaspoon soy sauce
$^1/_4$ teaspoon garlic powder
$^1/_4$ teaspoon salt
$^1/_4$ teaspoon celery salt
$^1/_4$ teaspoon onion salt

Combine tuna, cream cheese, mayonnaise, capers, horseradish, soy sauce, garlic powder, salt, celery salt and onion salt in mixer bowl, beating until mixed. Serve on toast points.

Yield: 10 to 12

Marinated Onions

$^1/_2$ cup vegetable oil
2 tablespoons fresh lemon juice
1 teaspoon salt
Freshly ground pepper to taste
Paprika to taste
$^1/_2$ teaspoon sugar
$^1/_4$ cup crumbled bleu cheese
2 cups thinly sliced sweet onions

Mix oil, lemon juice, salt, pepper, paprika and sugar in small bowl. Stir in cheese. Pour over onions in large bowl. Chill, covered, for 48 hours or longer. Serve with cocktail rye or pumpernickel bread.

Yield: 20 to 24 servings

STARTERS & BEVERAGES

Mustard Chicken Pâté with Ham and Olives

12 ounces boneless skinless chicken
breasts, chopped
2 shallots, cut into quarters
$^3/_4$ cup cottage cheese
2 eggs
$1^1/_2$ tablespoons country-style Dijon mustard
5 ounces whipping cream
2 ounces whole pimento-stuffed olives
5 ounces cooked ham, chopped

Rinse chicken and pat dry. Place chicken and shallots in food processor container fitted with steel blade.

Process just until smooth, scraping sides frequently. Add cottage cheese, eggs and Dijon mustard.

Process until mixed. Add whipping cream gradually, pulsing to blend; do not overmix. Fold in olives and ham.

Spoon into greased loaf pan; tap on counter to remove air bubbles. Place in bain-marie; cover with foil.

Bake at 325 degrees for 40 to 50 minutes or until set. Let stand until cool. Chill, covered, for 8 to 10 hours.

Invert onto serving platter; slice. Serve with sliced French bread and country-style Dijon mustard.

Yield: 12 to 15 servings

Authentic Guacamole

*This recipe was provided by Rick Bayless
of the Frontera Grill.*

$^1/_2$ small onion, finely chopped
Fresh hot green chiles to taste, stemmed,
seeded, finely chopped
1 ripe medium-large tomato, finely chopped
1 clove of garlic, finely chopped
10 sprigs of fresh coriander, chopped
3 ripe medium avocados
$^1/_2$ teaspoon salt
Juice of $^1/_2$ lime

Combine onion, chiles, tomato, garlic and coriander in bowl; mix well.

Cut avocados into halves lengthwise. Twist halves in opposite directions to loosen pulp from pits. Scoop out pits and reserve. Scrape avocado pulp from skins into bowl.

Mash avocado pulp. Stir in tomato mixture until a coarse thick mass forms. Add salt and lemon juice. Add reserved avocado pits to bowl. Cover with plastic wrap, pressing to surface of guacamole. Let stand for a few minutes to enhance flavors.

Uncover and spoon guacamole into serving bowl, discarding pits. Garnish with additional chopped onion, additional coriander, radish slices and crumbled cheese. Serve immediately.

Yield: 12 to 15 servings

Michael Jordan's Portobello Mushrooms

$^1/_2$ cup demi-glace
1 cup unsalted butter, chopped
1$^1/_2$ teaspoons Dijon mustard
1 teaspoon chopped fresh sage
$^1/_4$ teaspoon minced garlic
1$^1/_2$ teaspoons olive oil
1 bunch leeks, julienned

$^1/_2$ cup seasoned flour
4 cups canola oil
4 (4-ounce) portobello mushrooms
$^1/_2$ cup olive oil
Salt and pepper to taste
$^1/_4$ cup grated Romano cheese
$^1/_4$ cup chopped red bell pepper

Cook demi-glace in saucepan until reduced by $^1/_2$, stirring constantly. Add butter gradually, stirring constantly until blended. Remove from heat. Whisk in Dijon mustard.

Simmer sage and garlic in olive oil in saucepan. Stir into the mustard mixture. Season to taste.

Soak leeks in ice water in bowl; drain. Coat with flour. Heat canola oil in skillet to 350 degrees. Deep-fry leeks for 25 to 30 seconds; drain.

Brush mushrooms with olive oil; sprinkle with salt and pepper. Grill over hot coals until tender.

Drizzle $^1/_4$ cup sauce on a plate. Mound $^1/_4$ of the leeks over the sauce. Top with 1 mushroom. Sprinkle with 1 tablespoon of the Romano cheese and 1 tablespoon of the red pepper. Repeat the process with the remaining sauce, leeks, mushrooms, cheese and pepper.

Yield: 4 servings

Shrimp and Avocado Quesadillas

4 flour tortillas
2 cups shredded Monterey Jack cheese
12 shrimp, cooked, peeled
$^1/_3$ cup cilantro leaves
2 avocados
2 Roma tomatoes, chopped
$^1/_4$ cup chopped red onion
1 clove of garlic, minced
$1^1/_2$ teaspoons lime juice
$^1/_4$ teaspoon salt
$^1/_8$ teaspoon Tabasco sauce
$^1/_8$ teaspoon pepper

Fold tortillas into halves; place on baking sheet. Stuff each tortilla with $^1/_2$ cup cheese, 3 shrimp and $^1/_4$ of the cilantro.

Bake at 400 degrees for 10 minutes or until cheese melts.

Mash avocados in bowl with fork. Reserve 1 tablespoon tomato. Add remaining tomatoes, onion, garlic, lime juice, salt, Tabasco sauce and pepper to avocados and mix gently.

Cut each quesadilla into 3 wedges. Arrange on a serving platter. Top with additional cilantro and reserved tomato. Serve with guacamole.

Serve as a luncheon entrée over baby greens.

Yield: 12 servings

Hotel Ritz Champagne

3 to 4 ripe strawberries
1 teaspoon lemon juice
1 teaspoon Cognac
Dry Champagne

Combine strawberries, lemon juice and Cognac in blender container. Process until smooth.

Pour into Champagne glass. Fill with Champagne.

Yield: 1 serving

Champagne Punch

1 ice ring with orange slices
1 bottle Champagne, chilled
1 bottle Rhine wine, chilled
1/2 cup Cointreau
1/2 cup brandy

Place ice ring in punch bowl.
Pour Champagne, wine, Cointreau and brandy over ice ring and mix well.
Ladle into punch cups.

Yield: 10 to 12 servings

Crimson Royale

3/4 cup frozen cranberry juice cocktail concentrate, thawed
6 teaspoons cranberry liqueur
6 teaspoons orange liqueur
1 bottle Champagne or other sparkling wine
12 whole cranberries
6 orange slices, folded into halves

Measure 2 tablespoons cranberry concentrate, 1 teaspoon cranberry liqueur and 1 teaspoon orange liqueur into each of 6 Champagne flutes. Top with Champagne.
Thread 1 cranberry, 1 orange slice and 1 cranberry onto each of 6 bamboo skewers. Place atop flutes.

Yield: 6 servings

Daiquiri Punch

1 (6-ounce) can frozen strawberry daiquiri mix
1 (6-ounce) can frozen lemonade concentrate
1 (2-liter) bottle ginger ale
1 bottle Champagne

Combine daiquiri mix and lemonade concentrate in punch bowl. Rinse insides of cans with a small amount of water and add to punch bowl.

Add ginger ale and Champagne gradually and mix well.

Ladle into punch cups.

Yield: 8 servings

Eskimo Latté

1 cup freshly brewed espresso, chilled
1 cup cold 2% milk
1 cup crushed ice
1 teaspoon sugar
Whipped cream

Process coffee, milk, ice and sugar in blender until smooth.

Pour into glasses. Top with whipped cream.

May add Kahlúa for variety.

Yield: 2 servings

Lime Zest Cooler

The key to this drink is using underripe limes.

8 large dark-green limes
1 quart water
$^3/_4$ to 1 cup (or more) sugar

Remove limes' zest with very fine rasp-like grater; do not use citrus zester. Transfer zest to bowl. Wrap and chill limes for another use.

Add the water to bowl, rinsing grater over bowl to push any zest which may have clung to grater into bowl.

Let stand for 1 hour.

Strain zest mixture through fine mesh sieve, pressing firmly on solids to extract as much liquid as possible. Add sugar until desired degree of sweetness is reached, stirring until dissolved.

Chill, covered, until serving time. Serve over ice.

Yield: 4 to 5 servings

Margaritas

This famous drink is from the Frontera Grill.
Rub the rims of the glasses with a lime wedge,
then dip them in a dish of kosher salt.

$1^1/_4$ cups Lime Zest Cooler (at left)
1 cup tequila
$^1/_3$ cup Triple Sec
$^1/_4$ cup freshly squeezed lime juice
$^1/_8$ teaspoon salt
1 cup ice cubes
1 egg white (optional)

Combine Lime Zest Cooler, tequila, Triple Sec, lime juice and salt in bowl and mix well.

Let stand at room temperature for 30 minutes.

Combine tequila mixture, ice cubes and egg white in blender container just before serving.

Process for 30 to 45 seconds or just until ice is chopped and egg white is frothy.

Serve over cracked or crushed ice immediately.

Yield: 4 servings

Bucktown

Bucktown, a neighborhood due west of the trendy Lincoln Park area, got its name more than 150 years ago from the settlers who raised goats in their backyards along the Chicago River. At one time, Bucktown's traditional working-class residents were predominantly Polish. The charming cottages and coach houses they built between 1870 and 1919 are now being rehabbed and the neighborhood is slowly becoming more gentrified. Today Bucktown is comprised of Hispanics living side by side with the original Polish residents. Recent arrivals include young urban professionals of diverse backgrounds.

Bucktown also has a thriving community of artists along with Wicker Park, its neighbor to the south. Chicago's alternative art world can be found in the coffeehouses, galleries, bars and theaters that have sprung up in this area in recent years. The full flavor of these neighborhoods can also be sampled in their many restaurants. Ethnic foods of all types from Eastern European to South American are served, along with an eclectic mix from newly established proprietors.

These neighborhoods open their doors to full display during the Around the Coyote Art Fair, an annual event that celebrates the diversity and art that makes this area one of the most stimulating communities in Chicago.

The West Tower Building

Bucktown Brunch & Gallery Walk

Spinach and Sausage Frittata 42

Oatmeal Raisin Muffins 50

Assorted Fresh Fruit

Swedish Apple Coffee Cake 47

Bloody Marys

Spinach and Sausage Frittata

Breakfast & Breads

Saffron Crepes

2 pinches of saffron threads	2 to 3 tablespoons melted butter or
2 eggs	light olive oil
$^3/_4$ cup milk	1 cup unbleached flour
$^1/_2$ cup water	3 to 4 basil leaves, finely sliced
$^1/_2$ teaspoon salt	

Cover saffron threads with a spoonful of hot water in small bowl. Set aside.

Combine eggs, milk, $^1/_2$ cup water, salt, butter and flour in blender container. Process briefly; scrape side of blender.

Process for 10 seconds longer. Pour into large bowl. Stir in saffron and basil.

Let rest, covered, for 1 hour or longer. Bake crepes in crepe pan using manufacturer's directions.

To make batter by hand, cover saffron threads with a spoonful of hot water in small bowl. Set aside.

Beat eggs lightly in large bowl. Stir in milk, $^1/_2$ cup water, salt and butter or light olive oil. Whisk in flour.

Stir just enough to combine ingredients; strain. Stir in saffron and basil.

Let rest for 30 minutes. Bake crepes in crepe pan using manufacturer's directions.

Stack crepes to keep warm or prepare in advance, wrap in foil and store in refrigerator. Reheat, wrapped in foil, in oven.

Variation: Omit the basil and serve filled with sweetened ricotta cheese. Drizzle with a fresh blueberry or strawberry sauce.

These crepes are especially attractive, speckled with basil and tinted with the yellow hue of saffron. Serve warm with fresh ricotta cheese or an olive or artichoke paste.

Yield: 12 eight-inch crepes or 16 six-inch crepes

Spinach and Sausage Frittata

1 pound Italian sausage
¹/₄ cup olive oil
1 (10-ounce) package frozen
spinach, thawed, drained
8 ounces mushrooms
1 medium onion, chopped
6 eggs
³/₄ cup grated Parmesan cheese

2 cloves of garlic, minced
¹/₂ teaspoon dried basil
¹/₄ teaspoon marjoram
¹/₄ teaspoon salt
¹/₄ teaspoon freshly ground pepper
1 cup shredded mozzarella cheese
¹/₄ cup grated Parmesan cheese

Brown sausage in large skillet over medium heat; remove sausage and drain well.

Heat olive oil in skillet until a haze forms. Add spinach, mushrooms and onion. Sauté until onion is translucent. Remove from heat.

Combine eggs, ³/₄ cup Parmesan cheese, garlic, basil, marjoram, salt and pepper in bowl and mix well. Stir in sausage and mushroom mixture.

Pour into buttered 9-inch cast-iron skillet or pie plate. Sprinkle with mozzarella cheese and remaining ¹/₄ cup Parmesan cheese.

Bake at 350 degrees for 25 minutes or until set.

Yield: 4 to 5 servings

Lobster Benedict

1 cup sliced mushrooms
2 tablespoons butter or margarine
1 tablespoon white wine
2 (4- to 6-ounce) lobster tails
Salt and white pepper to taste
2 tablespoons butter or margarine
1 tablespoon white vinegar

4 eggs
2 sourdough English muffins, split,
   buttered, toasted
1¼ cups Quick Hollandaise Sauce
   (page 44)
Sliced mushrooms
4 sprigs of dillweed

Sauté 1 cup mushrooms in 2 tablespoons butter in a skillet until tender. Add wine. Simmer for 2 minutes, stirring occasionally. Remove from heat. Cover to keep warm.

Remove lobster meat from tails; cut into 1-inch medallions. Season with salt and white pepper. Sauté in 2 tablespoons butter in skillet for 1 minute on each side.

Add vinegar to boiling water in egg poacher. Poach eggs for 3 minutes or until done to taste.

Layer each muffin half with ¼ of the mushrooms, ¼ of the lobster meat, 1 egg and ¼ of the sauce. Top with additional sliced mushrooms and dillweed.

Yield: 2 servings

Quick Hollandaise Sauce

4 egg yolks
2 tablespoons lemon juice
$^1/_2$ cup melted butter

Combine egg yolks and lemon juice in blender container. Pulse until blended.

Add butter gradually, processing constantly at low speed until blended. Process at high speed until fluffy.

Serve immediately or keep warm in double boiler.

Yield: $^1/_2$ cup

Eggs Florentine

1 (10-ounce) package frozen chopped spinach, thawed, drained
4 cups small curd cottage cheese
6 eggs, lightly beaten
8 ounces sharp Cheddar cheese, shredded
3 tablespoons flour

Squeeze moisture from spinach. Combine with cottage cheese, eggs, Cheddar cheese and flour in bowl and mix well.

Spoon into greased 9x13-inch baking pan.

Bake at 350 degrees for 1 hour or until set and light brown.

Yield: 8 to 10 servings

Mexican Scrambled Eggs

10 corn tortillas, cut into thin strips
$^1/_4$ cup vegetable oil
1 bunch scallions, minced
1 red pepper, julienned
1 jalapeño, seeded, minced
4 plum tomatoes, chopped
3 cloves of garlic, minced
1 teaspoon cumin
3 tablespoons minced fresh cilantro
10 eggs, lightly beaten
2 tablespoons butter
Salt and pepper to taste
1 cup shredded Cheddar cheese

Fry tortillas strips in oil in skillet over medium-high heat until crisp. Drain on paper towel.

Pour off some of the remaining oil, leaving just enough to sauté the vegetables. Add scallions, red pepper and jalapeño to skillet.

Sauté for 3 minutes. Stir in tomatoes and garlic.

Sauté for 5 minutes. Sprinkle with cumin.

Sauté for 1 minute. Remove from heat. Stir in cilantro.

Scramble eggs in butter in skillet until done to taste. Stir in vegetable mixture. Season with salt and pepper. Sprinkle with cheese.

Serve with toasted English muffins.

Yield: 4 servings

Cheese Bake

8 slices bacon, chopped
1 cup chopped onion
2 eggs, lightly beaten
$^3/_4$ cup sour cream
12 ounces Swiss cheese, cut into $^1/_2$-inch cubes
1 unbaked (8-inch) pie shell

Fry bacon in skillet until crisp. Drain, reserving pan drippings.

Sauté onion in reserved pan drippings in skillet until tender; drain.

Combine eggs and sour cream in bowl and mix well. Stir in bacon, onion and Swiss cheese. Pour into pie shell.

Bake at 375 degrees for 25 to 30 minutes or until set. Serve immediately.

Yield: 6 to 8 servings

Harvey Nichols Tart

1 red bell pepper, julienned
1 to 2 tablespoons butter
1 large onion, sliced
1 baked (9-inch) tart shell
Dijon mustard to taste
4 ounces Stilton cheese, crumbled
Black olives, cut vertically into halves
$^1/_2$ cup half-and-half
2 eggs, lightly beaten
Salt and freshly ground pepper to taste
Grated Parmesan cheese to taste

Sauté red pepper in butter in skillet until tender.
Sweat onion in small skillet over low heat.
Spread bottom of tart shell with thin layer of Dijon mustard. Sprinkle with Stilton cheese; top with onion. Arrange red pepper and olives in decorative pattern over prepared layers.
Whisk half-and-half, eggs, salt and pepper in bowl until blended. Pour over prepared layers. Sprinkle with Parmesan cheese.
Bake at 375 degrees for 40 minutes or until set and brown.
Serve hot or warm.

Yield: 6 servings

Healthy Brunch French Toast

1 cup maple syrup
1 loaf French bread, cut into 8 slices
Egg substitute equivalent to 3 eggs
$1^1/_2$ cups skim milk
2 teaspoons vanilla extract
$^1/_2$ teaspoon cinnamon
$^3/_4$ teaspoon nutmeg

Spray baking pan with nonstick cooking spray. Pour syrup into pan. Arrange bread over syrup.
Combine egg substitute, skim milk, vanilla, cinnamon and $^1/_4$ teaspoon of the nutmeg in bowl and mix well. Pour over bread.
Chill, covered, for 8 to 10 hours. Sprinkle with remaining nutmeg.
Bake at 350 degrees for 40 to 45 minutes or until golden brown. Serve with additional warm maple syrup.

Yield: 8 servings

Swedish Apple Coffee Cake

1¹/₂ cups sugar
¹/₂ cup vegetable shortening
2 eggs
1 teaspoon vanilla extract
1¹/₂ cups flour
1 teaspoon cinnamon
1 teaspoon baking soda
Salt to taste
Ground cloves to taste
3 cups chopped peeled apples
¹/₂ cup chopped nuts
3 tablespoons butter
3 tablespoons brown sugar
2 tablespoons milk

Beat sugar, shortening, eggs and vanilla in mixer bowl until light and fluffy. Add sifted mixture of flour, cinnamon, baking soda, salt and cloves and mix well.

Fold in apples and nuts. Spoon into greased 9x9-inch baking pan.

Bake at 375 degrees for 1 hour.

Heat butter, brown sugar and milk in saucepan until brown sugar dissolves, stirring constantly. Drizzle over top of coffee cake.

Yield: 9 servings

Sour Cream Coffee Cake

2 tablespoons sugar
¹/₂ teaspoon cinnamon
1¹/₂ cups sugar
1 cup butter, softened
1 cup sour cream
2 eggs, beaten
1 teaspoon vanilla extract
2 cups flour
1 teaspoon baking powder
¹/₂ teaspoon baking soda
¹/₂ cup chopped nuts
Confectioners' sugar to taste

Combine 2 tablespoons sugar and cinnamon in bowl and mix well.

Beat 1¹/₂ cups sugar and butter in mixer bowl until light and fluffy. Add sour cream, eggs and vanilla and mix well. Stir in flour, baking powder and baking soda.

Layer sour cream mixture, nuts and sugar and cinnamon mixture one-half at a time in greased 9x13-inch baking pan.

Bake at 350 degrees for 40 minutes. Cool in pan on wire rack for 20 minutes. Sprinkle with confectioners' sugar.

Yield: 15 servings

Swedish Pancakes

1^1/$_4$ cups flour
1 tablespoon sugar
^{1}/$_2$ teaspoon salt
2^1/$_2$ cups skim milk
3 eggs
2 tablespoons melted butter
3 tablespoons butter
^{1}/$_4$ cup confectioners' sugar
Seasonal berries

Sift flour, sugar and salt together.

Whisk 1 cup of the skim milk and eggs in bowl until blended. Add flour mixture gradually, whisking constantly. Whisk in remaining 1^1/$_2$ cups skim milk and 2 tablespoons melted butter until blended.

Heat ^{1}/$_2$ teaspoon of the butter in a skillet until hot. Pour ^{1}/$_4$ cup batter into skillet; rotate skillet to spread batter evenly over bottom.

Bake for 1 minute or until golden brown; turn pancake.

Bake for 1 minute longer. Transfer to a heated serving platter. Repeat process with remaining butter and batter.

Sprinkle each pancake with confectioners' sugar and fold into halves just before serving. Top with berries of your choice.

May prepare pancakes in advance and store, wrapped in plastic wrap, in freezer. Reheat, wrapped in foil, at 350 degrees for 5 to 7 minutes.

Yield: 6 servings

Sour Cream Waffles

2 eggs
2 tablespoons sugar
1 teaspoon baking soda
^{1}/$_2$ teaspoon salt
1 cup sour cream
1 cup milk
3 tablespoons vegetable oil
1 teaspoon vanilla extract
1^1/$_2$ cups flour

Beat eggs in mixer bowl until light and fluffy. Add sugar, baking soda and salt and mix well.

Beat in sour cream until blended. Add milk, oil and vanilla and mix well. Add flour, mixing until blended.

Let stand for 30 minutes.

Pour approximately ^{1}/$_2$ cup batter onto hot waffle iron. Bake using manufacturer's directions. Repeat process with remaining batter.

Serve with sliced fresh fruit and almond butter.

Yield: 4 to 6 servings

English Muffin Bread

Vegetable oil
Cornmeal
2 cups milk or half-and-half
$^1/_2$ cup water
6 cups (about) bread flour
2 envelopes dry yeast, at room temperature
1 tablespoon sugar
2 teaspoons salt
$^1/_4$ teaspoon baking soda

Brush sides and bottoms of two 5x9-inch loaf pans with oil; sprinkle with cornmeal.

Heat milk and water in saucepan until lukewarm or to 115 degrees.

Combine 3 cups of the bread flour, yeast, sugar, salt and baking soda in bowl and mix well. Add milk mixture, beating until blended. Add enough remaining flour to make a stiff dough. Divide dough into 2 equal portions.

Shape each portion into a loaf in prepared pan; sprinkle with cornmeal.

Let rise, covered with tea towel, in warm place for 1 hour or longer.

Bake at 400 degrees for 25 minutes. Invert onto wire rack to cool.

Yield: 24 servings

Old-Fashioned English Scones

2 cups flour
4 teaspoons baking powder
2 teaspoons sugar
$^1/_2$ teaspoon salt
$^1/_4$ cup butter
2 eggs, beaten
$^1/_3$ cup half-and-half

Sift flour, baking powder, sugar and salt into bowl and mix well. Cut in butter until crumbly. Stir in eggs and half-and-half.

Knead on lightly floured surface several times. Shape into ball. Pat $^1/_2$ inch thick on lightly floured surface; cut into $2^1/_2$- to 3-inch rounds. Arrange on buttered baking sheet.

Bake at 425 degrees for 12 to 15 minutes or until golden brown. Serve warm.

May cut into halves before serving. Serve with butter, jam and clotted cream.

Do not substitute margarine for butter in this recipe.

Yield: 10 servings

Banana Cream Chocolate Chip Muffins

1 cup packed brown sugar
$^{1}/_{2}$ cup butter, softened
3 ounces cream cheese, softened
2 bananas, mashed
$^{1}/_{4}$ cup sour cream
1 egg
1$^{1}/_{2}$ cups flour
$^{3}/_{4}$ cup chocolate chips
1 teaspoon baking soda
1 teaspoon baking powder
$^{1}/_{2}$ teaspoon salt

Beat brown sugar, butter and cream cheese in mixer bowl until creamy. Add bananas, sour cream and egg and mix well.

Combine flour, chocolate chips, baking soda and baking powder in bowl and mix well. Make a well in center of ingredients. Pour banana mixture into well and mix just until moistened. Fill greased muffin cups $^{2}/_{3}$ full.

Bake at 325 degrees for 20 to 25 minutes or until muffins test done.

Yield: 12 servings

Oatmeal Raisin Muffins

1 cup buttermilk
1 cup quick-cooking oats
$^{1}/_{2}$ cup raisins
1 cup flour
1 teaspoon baking powder
1 teaspoon cinnamon
$^{3}/_{4}$ teaspoon salt
$^{1}/_{2}$ teaspoon baking soda
$^{1}/_{4}$ teaspoon ground cloves
$^{1}/_{3}$ cup butter, softened
$^{1}/_{4}$ cup packed light brown sugar
1 egg
1 tablespoon honey

Combine buttermilk, oats and raisins in bowl and mix well. Let stand for 20 minutes.

Sift flour, baking powder, cinnamon, salt, baking soda and cloves together.

Beat butter and brown sugar in mixing bowl until light and fluffy. Add egg and honey, beating until blended.

Add flour mixture alternately with buttermilk mixture, stirring after each addition just until moistened. Spoon into greased muffin cups.

Bake at 400 degrees for 30 minutes.

Yield: 12 servings

Old-Fashioned Cinnamon Rolls

2 envelopes dry yeast
$^1/_2$ cup lukewarm water
$1^1/_2$ cups milk
$1^1/_2$ cups butter
$^1/_4$ cup sugar
$^1/_2$ teaspoon salt
4 eggs, beaten

$8^1/_4$ cups (about) flour
1 cup sugar
1 tablespoon cinnamon
$^1/_2$ cup melted butter
4 cups confectioners' sugar
6 tablespoons warm water
1 teaspoon vanilla extract

Soften yeast in lukewarm water in bowl and mix well.

Heat milk, $1^1/_2$ cups butter and $^1/_4$ cup sugar in saucepan until butter melts, stirring frequently. Cool to lukewarm. Stir in salt and yeast mixture. Add eggs and mix well.

Place 8 cups of the flour in large bowl. Add yeast mixture, stirring until dough clings together. Knead for 5 minutes or until smooth and elastic, adding remaining flour as needed.

Place dough in greased bowl, turning to coat surface.

Let rise, covered, for 1 hour or until doubled in bulk. Punch dough down.

Chill, covered, for 3 to 10 hours. May store in refrigerator for up to 3 days.

Combine 1 cup sugar and cinnamon in bowl and mix well.

Divide dough into 8 portions. Work with 1 portion at a time, storing remaining portions in refrigerator. Roll each portion into 9x12-inch rectangle on lightly floured surface.

Brush with 1 tablespoon of the melted butter; sprinkle with 2 tablespoons of the cinnamon and sugar mixture.

Roll as for jelly roll, sealing edge. Cut into eight $1^1/_2$-inch slices. Place cut side up $^1/_2$ inch apart in greased 8-inch baking pan; each pan will hold 16 slices. Repeat process with remaining dough.

Let rise for 45 minutes or until almost doubled in bulk.

Bake at 375 degrees for 20 to 25 minutes or until golden brown.

Combine confectioners' sugar, warm water and vanilla in bowl and mix well. Drizzle evenly over rolls.

May be baked, glazed and frozen for future use.

Yield: 64 servings

Apple Bread

2 cups sugar
1 cup vegetable oil
3 eggs, lightly beaten
2 teaspoons vanilla extract
3 cups flour
1 teaspoon salt
1 teaspoon cinnamon
1 teaspoon baking soda
3 cups chopped apples
1 cup nuts (optional)

Combine sugar, oil, eggs and vanilla in bowl and mix well. Stir in mixture of flour, salt, cinnamon and baking soda. Fold in apples and nuts.

Spoon into 2 greased and floured 5x9-inch loaf pans.

Bake at 325 degrees for 50 to 60 minutes or until loaves test done.

Yield: 24 servings

Banana Bread

1 cup all-purpose flour
1 cup whole wheat flour
1 teaspoon baking powder
$^1/_2$ teaspoon salt
$^1/_2$ teaspoon baking soda
1 teaspoon cinnamon
$^1/_2$ teaspoon ground cloves
$^1/_4$ teaspoon nutmeg
1 cup sugar
$^1/_2$ cup melted butter
2 eggs, slightly beaten
1 cup mashed very ripe bananas
$^1/_2$ cup chopped walnuts (optional)

Sift all-purpose flour, whole wheat flour, baking powder, salt, baking soda, cinnamon, cloves and nutmeg together.

Cream sugar and melted butter in a mixer bowl until light and fluffy. Beat in eggs. Add the bananas and mix well.

Blend in flour mixture. Fold in walnuts. Pour into greased and floured 5x9-inch loaf pan.

Bake at 350 degrees for 50 to 55 minutes or until loaf tests done.

Let stand until cool. Cut into slices.

Yield: 12 servings

Blueberry Lemon Bread

4 cups flour
1 tablespoon baking soda
1 teaspoon salt
1 teaspoon baking powder
2 cups sugar
$^3/_4$ cup lemon juice
$^1/_2$ cup melted butter
$^1/_4$ cup orange juice
2 eggs, beaten
2 tablespoons grated lemon peel
3 to 4 cups fresh blueberries
$1^1/_2$ cups whole or chopped pecans

Combine flour, baking soda, salt and baking powder in bowl and mix well.

Combine sugar, lemon juice, butter, orange juice, eggs and lemon peel in bowl and mix well. Add dry ingredients, stirring just until moistened. Fold in blueberries and pecans. Spoon into 2 greased 5x9-inch loaf pans.

Bake at 350 degrees for 1 hour or until golden brown. Flavor is best if baked just until slightly underdone; wooden pick inserted in center should be almost clean.

May substitute frozen blueberries for fresh blueberries, but the flavor is compromised. May freeze for future use.

Yield: 24 servings

Grandmother's Pumpkin Bread

3 cups sugar
1 cup corn oil
4 eggs, beaten
1 (16-ounce) can pumpkin
$3^1/_2$ cups flour
2 teaspoons baking soda
2 teaspoons salt
1 teaspoon baking powder
1 teaspoon nutmeg
1 teaspoon cinnamon
1 teaspoon allspice
$^1/_2$ teaspoon ground cloves
$^2/_3$ cup water

Combine sugar, corn oil and eggs in bowl and mix well. Stir in pumpkin until blended.

Sift flour, baking soda, salt, baking powder, nutmeg, cinnamon, allspice and cloves together. Add to the pumpkin mixture and mix well. Stir in water. Spoon into 8 greased miniature loaf pans or 2 greased 5x9-inch loaf pans.

Bake at 350 degrees for 1 hour or until loaves test done.

Yield: 24 servings

Focaccia

1 tablespoon dry yeast	1 teaspoon salt
1^1/$_4$ cups lukewarm water	1 egg, lightly beaten
^{1}/$_3$ cup nonfat dry milk powder	3^1/$_2$ to 4 cups bread flour
^{1}/$_4$ cup olive oil	^{1}/$_4$ cup olive oil
2 tablespoons sugar	1 teaspoon kosher salt

Soften yeast in lukewarm water in bowl and mix well. Stir in milk powder, ^{1}/$_4$ cup olive oil, sugar, salt and egg until blended. Add 3 cups of the bread flour gradually, stirring well after each addition. Add ^{1}/$_2$ cup of the remaining flour, mixing until smooth. Sprinkle some of the remaining ^{1}/$_2$ cup flour on a board or hard surface.

Knead the dough on the board, kneading in just enough flour until dough is smooth and nonsticky. Knead until dough is smooth and elastic. Place dough in greased bowl, turning to coat surface. Let rise, covered with plastic wrap, in warm place for 90 minutes or until doubled in bulk. Punch dough down. Let rise for 40 minutes or until doubled in bulk. Punch dough down. Divide into 2 portions. Let rest for 10 minutes.

Pat each portion into an oval on a baking sheet sprayed with nonstick cooking spray. Brush the surface of each oval with half the ^{1}/$_4$ cup olive oil and sprinkle with half the kosher salt. Make indentions over entire surface of both ovals with fingertips; do not make holes.

Let rise, covered with tea towel, in warm place for 30 minutes or until doubled in bulk. Press indentions with fingertips into dough again.

Bake at 375 degrees for 20 to 25 minutes or until as brown and crisp as desired.

Garlic and Parmesan Focaccia–Add 6 to 8 cloves of crushed garlic to the olive oil that is used to brush over the dough and sprinkle with grated Parmesan cheese to taste. *Green Onion Focaccia*–Bake the loaves for 15 minutes. Sprinkle with mixture of 1 bunch finely chopped green onions and 2 tablespoons dark olive oil. Bake using the remaining directions. *Vidalia Onion Focaccia*–Sprinkle tops of the unbaked loaves with a mixture of thinly sliced vidalia onions and olive oil. *Tomato-Basil Focaccia*–Top unbaked loaves with ^{1}/$_4$-inch slices Roma tomatoes and fresh basil leaves. Brush the tomatoes and basil with olive oil.

Yield: 12 servings

Three-Cheese Bread

2 envelopes dry yeast
3 tablespoons sugar
2 teaspoons salt
4 cups flour, sifted
$1^1/2$ cups low-fat milk
1 tablespoon unsalted butter
$^1/2$ cup shredded Swiss cheese
$^1/2$ cup shredded Cheddar cheese
$^1/2$ cup freshly grated Parmesan cheese

Combine yeast, sugar, salt and 2 cups of the flour in bowl and mix well.

Heat milk and butter in saucepan to 110 degrees. Add to yeast mixture gradually, beating until blended. Beat for 1 to 2 minutes longer. Stir in Swiss cheese, Cheddar cheese, Parmesan cheese and remaining flour gradually, stirring until stiff dough forms.

Let rise, covered, in warm place for 1 hour or until doubled in bulk. Punch dough down. Shape into loaf in greased 5x9-inch loaf pan.

Bake at 350 degrees for 45 minutes. Lay a piece of foil over top of loaf; do not seal.

Bake for 15 minutes longer or until loaf sounds hollow when tapped with flat side of knife blade. Invert onto wire rack to cool.

Yield: 12 servings

Irish Soda Bread

3 cups flour
$^2/3$ cup sugar
1 tablespoon baking powder
1 teaspoon baking soda
1 teaspoon salt
$1^1/2$ cups raisins
$1^3/4$ cups buttermilk
2 eggs, beaten
2 tablespoons melted butter

Sift flour, sugar, baking powder, baking soda and salt into bowl and mix well. Stir in raisins.

Combine buttermilk, eggs and butter in bowl and mix well. Stir into flour mixture until mixed. Spoon into 2 greased miniature loaf pans or one 5x9-inch loaf pan.

Bake at 350 degrees for 1 hour or until loaves test done. Invert onto wire rack to cool.

Yield: 12 servings

Bantry Brown Bread

1 cup all-purpose flour
$^1/_4$ cup sugar
2 teaspoons baking powder
1 teaspoon baking soda
1 teaspoon salt
2 cups whole wheat flour
$^1/_4$ cup currants
$^1/_4$ cup shortening
$1^1/_4$ cups buttermilk
2 tablespoons sugar
1 tablespoon water

Sift all-purpose flour, $^1/_4$ cup sugar, baking powder, baking soda and salt into medium bowl. Stir in whole wheat flour and currants. Cut in shortening with pastry blender or fork until crumbly. Stir in buttermilk.

Knead 10 times on lightly floured pastry cloth or board. Shape into 7-inch round loaf. Place on nonstick baking sheet. Cut a cross in top of dough.

Bake at 375 degrees for 40 minutes. Remove from oven.

Mix 2 tablespoons sugar and water in small saucepan. Bring to a boil. Brush over hot loaf.

Bake for 5 minutes longer or until golden brown.

Yield: 12 servings

Mexican Corn Bread

$1^1/_2$ cups yellow self-rising cornmeal
1 cup flour
$^1/_4$ cup sugar
$1^1/_2$ teaspoons baking powder
1 teaspoon salt
1 (16-ounce) can cream-style corn
1 cup cottage cheese
1 cup buttermilk
$^2/_3$ cup vegetable oil
2 eggs
$^1/_2$ cup shredded sharp Cheddar cheese or
Monterey Jack cheese
1 (4-ounce) can chopped green chiles
2 tablespoons minced onion
1 cup shredded sharp Cheddar cheese (optional)

Combine cornmeal, flour, sugar, baking powder and salt in bowl and mix well. Gently stir in corn, cottage cheese, buttermilk, oil and eggs.

Spoon half of the batter into greased 9x13-inch baking pan. Spread with mixture of $^1/_2$ cup Cheddar cheese, green chiles and onion. Top with remaining batter. Sprinkle with 1 cup Cheddar cheese.

Bake at 425 degrees for 40 minutes.

May substitute regular cornmeal for self-rising cornmeal and increase baking powder to 1 tablespoon.

Yield: 10 to 12 servings

Swedish Rye Bread

2 cakes yeast
1 cup lukewarm water
1 teaspoon sugar
1$^{1}/_{2}$ cups all-purpose flour
2 cups milk
1 cup water
5 tablespoons melted margarine
3 cups rye flour
1 cup all-purpose flour

$^{1}/_{2}$ cup packed brown sugar
$^{1}/_{4}$ cup sugar
1 tablespoon salt
1 teaspoon anise seeds
1$^{1}/_{2}$ teaspoons caraway seeds
$^{1}/_{2}$ cup molasses
3 tablespoons dark corn syrup
3$^{1}/_{2}$ cups all-purpose flour

Dissolve yeast in 1 cup lukewarm water in medium bowl. Add 1 teaspoon sugar and 1$^{1}/_{2}$ cups all-purpose flour. Set aside.

Scald milk in saucepan. Stir in 1 cup water and margarine. Set aside.

Combine rye flour, 1 cup all-purpose flour, brown sugar, $^{1}/_{4}$ cup sugar, salt, anise seeds, caraway seeds, molasses and corn syrup in large bowl; mix well. Stir in milk mixture. Add yeast mixture, mixing well until soft dough forms.

Sift 3$^{1}/_{2}$ cups all-purpose flour onto a board. Place dough on the board. Knead and fold dough to incorporate all the flour. Place in large greased bowl. Cover and let rise in a warm place for 2 hours or until doubled in bulk. Punch dough down and shape into 6 small loaves. Place in nonstick loaf pans. Let rise for 30 to 60 minutes or until 1 inch above rim of pans.

Bake at 350 degrees for 45 minutes or until loaves test done. Remove to a wire rack to cool.

Yield: 24 servings

BREAKFAST & BREADS

Printer's Row

The area just south of the Chicago Loop was once a thriving industrial park and the center of Midwest publishing. After the Dearborn Street Train Station opened in 1885, many printers and publishers built plants in this area because of its access to the railroads. This restored train depot, once a point of entry for arriving immigrants, remains a prominent landmark in the neighborhood.

In 1983, investors began renovating the run-down yet sturdy loft and office buildings in the south Loop. River City, a combination of apartments, restaurants, offices, ice-skating rink and marina, was built in 1984 along the Chicago River and has become an architecturally significant site. Soon after, other restaurants, shops and businesses moved into the area.

Today, Printer's Row is a thriving urban neighborhood enclave, complete with many landmark buildings that are listed in the National Register of Historic Places.

Dearborn Station train depot

Heartland Dinner

Mushroom Barley Soup 68

Stuffed Pork Tenderloin 162

New Potatoes with Herbs 136

Sautéed Squash 141

Apple Torte with Butterscotch Sauce 223

Mushroom Barley Soup

Soups

Black Bean Soup

1 pound dried black beans
2 teaspoons salt
1 cup cooked white rice
$^1/_2$ cup chopped onion
$^1/_2$ cup olive oil
$^1/_4$ cup white or cider vinegar
6 cloves of garlic, crushed

2 teaspoons cumin
2 teaspoons oregano
2 tablespoons white or cider vinegar
2 medium onions, chopped
1 medium green bell pepper,
chopped
$^1/_3$ cup olive oil

Sort and rinse beans. Soak in 2 quarts water in large pot overnight.

Pour off water until beans are just covered. Add salt. Bring to a boil. Simmer over low heat for 3 hours or until beans are tender.

Combine rice, $^1/_2$ cup onion, $^1/_2$ cup olive oil and $^1/_4$ cup vinegar in large bowl. Marinate for 3 hours or until beans have finished cooking.

Mix garlic, cumin, oregano and 2 tablespoons vinegar in small bowl; set aside.

Sauté 2 onions and green pepper in $^1/_3$ cup olive oil in skillet over low heat. Add spice mixture and mix well. Add to beans. Cook over low heat for 15 minutes or until heated through.

Ladle into bowls. Add 1 spoonful rice mixture to each bowl.

Yield: 6 to 8 servings

SOUPS

Cold Two-Melon Soup

3 cups coarsely chopped cantaloupe
3 cups coarsely chopped honeydew melon
$^1/_3$ cup fresh lime juice
2 cups fresh orange juice
$^1/_4$ cup honey
2 cups dry Champagne
1 cup whipping cream, whipped
8 strawberries

Chop finely half the cantaloupe and honeydew; set aside.

Combine remaining cantaloupe, honeydew, lime juice, orange juice and honey in blender container. Process for several seconds. Pour into large bowl.

Add reserved cantaloupe, honeydew and Champagne. Chill, covered, until serving time.

Pour into iced sherbet dishes. Top with whipped cream and strawberries.

Yield: 8 servings

Chilled White Gazpacho

$1^1/_2$ seedless cucumbers, peeled,
cut into small chunks
1 cup sour cream
$2^1/_2$ cups plain low-fat yogurt
1 tablespoon sugar, or to taste
1 teaspoon lemon juice
$^1/_2$ teaspoon salt
$^1/_8$ teaspoon hot pepper sauce, or to taste
$^1/_8$ teaspoon Worcestershire sauce, or to taste
1 tomato, peeled, seeded, chopped
4 green onions, ends trimmed, chopped
1 red or yellow bell pepper, roasted,
peeled, chopped
$^1/_2$ cup watercress, stems trimmed
$^1/_4$ cup chopped fresh chives
$^1/_3$ cup toasted sliced almonds
12 cloves of garlic, roasted, peeled

Process cucumbers in food processor or blender until puréed.

Add sour cream, yogurt, sugar, lemon juice, salt, hot pepper sauce and Worcestershire sauce. Process until mixed.

Pour into nonreactive bowl. Chill, covered, for 1 hour or longer.

Place tomato, green onions, red pepper, watercress, chives, almonds and garlic in separate small dishes. Arrange dishes on platter.

Adjust seasonings in soup. Ladle soup into bowls or soup plates. Serve toppings separately.

Yield: 6 servings

SOUPS

Strawberry Soup

1 cup strained puréed strawberries
$^1/_2$ cup apple juice
$^1/_2$ cup yogurt
$^1/_8$ teaspoon salt, or to taste
Sugar to taste
Sliced strawberries

Combine puréed strawberries, apple juice, yogurt, salt and sugar in large bowl and mix well. Chill until serving time.

Ladle into bowls. Top with a few sliced strawberries.

Yield: 2 servings

Beer Cheese Soup

$^1/_4$ cup minced onion
2 tablespoons minced carrot
$^1/_4$ cup minced green bell pepper
3 tablespoons butter
2 tablespoons flour
$3^1/_2$ cups chicken broth
8 ounces Cheddar cheese, shredded
$1^1/_2$ cups beer
Salt and pepper to taste

Sauté onion, carrot and green pepper in butter in skillet for 5 minutes.

Stir in flour. Sauté for 2 minutes.

Add chicken broth and mix well. Simmer for 5 minutes.

Add cheese and beer. Cook until cheese is melted, stirring constantly.

Season with salt and pepper.

Yield: 4 servings

SOUPS

Jerusalem Artichoke Soup
with Garlic Croutons

2^1/$_2$ pounds Jerusalem artichokes,
peeled, thickly sliced
2 tablespoons lemon juice
2 tablespoons unsalted butter
1 large onion, coarsely chopped
2 cloves of garlic, minced
2 quarts chicken stock or canned
low-sodium chicken broth
^{1}/$_2$ teaspoon salt

^{1}/$_4$ teaspoon white pepper
1^1/$_2$ cups whipping cream
2 teaspoons lemon juice
12 (^{1}/$_2$-inch) diagonal sourdough
baguette slices
1^1/$_2$ tablespoons vegetable oil
1 clove of garlic, cut into halves
Croutons
2 tablespoons minced fresh chives

Combine artichokes with cold water to cover and 2 tablespoons lemon juice in large bowl.

Melt butter in large enameled cast-iron soup pot. Add onion. Cook over medium-high heat for 7 minutes or until translucent, stirring frequently. Add minced garlic. Cook for 1 minute, stirring constantly.

Drain artichokes and add to onion mixture. Add chicken stock, salt and pepper. Bring to a boil over high heat; reduce heat to medium. Simmer for 35 minutes or until artichokes are tender.

Purée soup in batches in blender until smooth. Return to soup pot. At this point, soup may be refrigerated for up to 1 day before finishing.

Bring soup to a boil over high heat. Cook for 5 minutes or until slightly thickened; reduce heat to low. Stir in whipping cream. Add 2 teaspoons lemon juice. Adjust seasonings. Set aside and keep warm.

Brush baguette slices with oil. Place on baking sheet. Bake at 350 degrees for 5 minutes or until lightly browned. Rub each crouton with garlic half.

Ladle into tureen or shallow bowls. Top with croutons and chives.

Yield: 12 servings

Curried Lentil and Spinach Soup

4 teaspoons olive oil
1 white onion, chopped
2 cloves of garlic, chopped
2 teaspoons minced ginger
4 teaspoons hot curry powder
$1^1/_2$ teaspoons ground cumin
1 cup lentils
$2^1/_2$ cups chicken broth
$2^1/_2$ cups water
$1^1/_2$ cups chopped seeded tomatoes
2 cups packed spinach
Juice of 1 lemon
Salt and pepper to taste

Heat olive oil in medium saucepan over low heat. Add onion. Sauté until softened.

Add garlic, ginger, curry powder and cumin. Sauté for 2 minutes.

Add lentils, chicken broth and water. Bring to a boil. Simmer, covered, for 25 minutes.

Stir in tomatoes and spinach. Simmer for 5 minutes.

Add lemon juice, salt and pepper.

Yield: 4 servings

Creamy Carrot with Dill Soup

2 tablespoons butter
1 cup chopped onion
5 cups sliced peeled carrots
5 cups chicken stock
$1/_2$ teaspoon salt
$1/_4$ teaspoon white pepper
$1/_4$ cup ricotta cheese
$1/_4$ cup port wine
3 tablespoons chopped fresh dill
Dill for garnish

Melt butter in medium saucepan over low heat. Add onion. Sauté for 5 minutes or until translucent.

Add carrots, chicken stock, salt and pepper. Simmer, covered, over low heat for 30 minutes, stirring occasionally.

Purée hot carrot mixture and ricotta cheese in blender or food processor until smooth. Return to saucepan.

Bring to a boil over medium heat. Stir in wine and dill.

Serve immediately. Garnish with dill.

Yield: 6 servings

Curried Zucchini and Potato Soup

From the kitchen of Mayor and Mrs. Richard M. Daley

4 large zucchini, chopped or sliced
2 onions, chopped
$^1/_2$ teaspoon curry powder
$^1/_2$ cup chopped parsley
4 cups chicken broth
1 cup cooked potatoes
$^1/_2$ cup light cream
Salt to taste
$^1/_2$ cup plain yogurt
Chopped watercress or parsley

Combine zucchini, onions, curry powder, $^1/_2$ cup parsley and chicken broth in large saucepan. Cook until vegetables are tender.

Purée 1 cup at a time with potatoes in blender. Stir in cream and salt.

Serve hot or cold. Top with dollop of yogurt. Sprinkle with watercress.

May be frozen before cream is added. Defrost and serve cold with cream added, or heat and then add cream.

Yield: 8 servings

Mushroom Barley Soup

2 leeks
$^1/_4$ cup clarified butter
$2^1/_2$ to 3 cups sliced mushrooms
$^1/_2$ cup chopped onion
$^1/_2$ cup chopped celery
$^1/_2$ cup half-moon slices carrot
4 cloves of garlic, crushed
4 cups beef stock or broth
2 teaspoons chopped fresh rosemary
2 teaspoons chopped fresh thyme
1 cup cooked barley
Salt and pepper to taste
2 teaspoons chopped fresh cilantro

Cut leeks into halves lengthwise; cut halves into half-moon slices.

Heat butter in stockpot. Add mushrooms, onion, leeks, celery, carrot and garlic in order listed, stirring after each addition. Sauté for 5 minutes; do not brown.

Add beef stock. Bring to a simmer. Simmer until vegetables are tender. Add rosemary, thyme, barley, salt and pepper. Cook just until heated through. Top with cilantro.

Note: To yield $^1/_4$ cup clarified butter, melt 1 stick butter in pan. Skim off and discard white milk solids that form around top and sides of pan; some will sink to the bottom. Pour off and use the remaining clear yellow butterfat.

Variation: Can use an assortment of mushrooms including shiitake and portobello mushrooms.

Yield: 1 serving

Potato-Leek Soup in Bread Bowls

$^1/_2$ teaspoon olive oil
1 medium onion, finely chopped
2 large leeks, thinly sliced
1 shallot, minced
2 large potatoes, peeled,
finely chopped
4 cups chicken broth
2 tablespoons finely chopped
fresh dill

Salt and pepper to taste
4 unsliced round loaves of bread
4 teaspoons olive oil
2 cloves of garlic, crushed
3 tablespoons grated
Parmesan cheese
$^1/_8$ teaspoon grated nutmeg,
or to taste
Chopped parsley

Heat $^1/_2$ teaspoon olive oil in large pot over medium heat. Add onion, leeks and shallot. Cook, covered, for 10 to 12 minutes or until tender, stirring occasionally.

Add potatoes, chicken broth, dill, salt and pepper. Bring to a boil; reduce heat to low. Simmer, covered, for 20 minutes or until potatoes are tender.

Cut lids from bread with small sharp knife, leaving $^3/_4$-inch edge. Hollow out centers of bread. Reserve removed bread for croutons if desired. Brush inside each loaf with 1 teaspoon olive oil. Rub insides with garlic; sprinkle with cheese. Place loaves and lids on baking sheet. Bake at 350 degrees for 12 to 15 minutes or until cheese melts.

Strain soup through a sieve into another pot. Place solids in blender or food processor container. Add 1 cup of the hot soup. Process until smooth. Whisk back into remaining soup to thicken. Stir in nutmeg. Cook until heated through.

Spoon hot soup into bread bowls. Top with parsley.

Yield: 4 servings

SOUPS

Pumpkin Soup

$^1/_4$ cup butter or margarine
1 large onion, chopped
1 leek, chopped
1 pound canned or homemade
pumpkin purée
5 cups chicken broth
$^1/_4$ teaspoon white pepper
1 teaspoon salt

$^1/_2$ teaspoon curry powder
$^1/_4$ teaspoon nutmeg
$^1/_4$ teaspoon ginger
1 bay leaf
1 cup half-and-half
1 cup sour cream
$^1/_2$ cup chopped chives

Melt butter in medium saucepan. Add onion and leek. Sauté until tender.

Stir in pumpkin purée, chicken broth, pepper, salt, curry powder, nutmeg, ginger and bay leaf. Bring to a boil; reduce heat. Simmer for 15 minutes. Remove bay leaf.

Purée soup mixture in blender or food processor. Return to saucepan. Add half-and-half. Soup may be served at this point or refrigerated or frozen.

Serve hot or cold. Top with dollop of sour cream. Sprinkle with chives.

May hollow out a pumpkin and fill it with soup. Heat at 350 degrees for 45 minutes and serve from the pumpkin.

Note: To prepare a pumpkin purée, cut a fresh 3-pound pumpkin into cubes. Combine cubes with water to cover in a saucepan. Bring to a boil; reduce heat. Simmer, covered, for 20 minutes or until fork-tender. Drain and press through a sieve.

Yield: 6 to 8 servings

SOUPS

Roasted Squash Bisque

8 (^{1}/$_2$-inch) slices French baguette
^{1}/$_3$ cup freshly grated Parmesan cheese
1 (2-pound) acorn squash, peeled, chopped
1 (2-pound) butternut squash, peeled, chopped
1 medium onion, chopped
3 tablespoons vegetable oil
1 quart chicken stock
1 bay leaf
2 sprigs of fresh thyme
1 cup whipping cream
Salt and freshly ground pepper to taste

Top bread with cheese. Brown under broiler and set aside.

Sauté squash and onion in oil in large pot. Add chicken stock, bay leaf and thyme. Simmer for 15 minutes. Remove and discard bay leaf and thyme.

Strain solids from pot. Purée with a small amount of hot soup in food processor or blender. Return to pot. Adjust texture by adding additional chicken stock or water if needed.

Stir in whipping cream gradually. Cook until heated through. Season with salt and pepper.

Top each serving with Parmesan bread.

Yield: 6 to 8 servings

Autumn Squash and Apple Bisque

^{1}/$_4$ cup butter
1 large yellow onion, chopped
^{1}/$_2$ teaspoon ginger
^{1}/$_2$ teaspoon cinnamon
1 quart chicken stock or broth
^{1}/$_2$ cup dry sherry
2 medium butternut squash, peeled, seeded, chopped
2^1/$_2$ apples, cored, peeled, chopped
^{1}/$_2$ cup whipping cream
Salt and cayenne to taste

Melt butter in heavy Dutch oven over medium heat. Add onion, ginger and cinnamon.

Sauté until onion is transparent. Add chicken stock, sherry, squash and apples. Bring to a boil. Simmer until squash and apples are tender. Cool slightly.

Purée in batches in blender. Stir in whipping cream, salt and cayenne. Return to Dutch oven. Cook until heated through.

Yield: 6 servings

SOUPS

Thick and Hearty Soup

4 precooked spiced turkey
sausage slices
2 tablespoons olive oil
³/₄ cup sliced carrot
³/₄ cup chopped celery
1 small yellow onion, chopped
1 tablespoon fresh rosemary
1 tablespoon olive oil
3 cups chicken broth
1 teaspoon thyme

¹/₂ teaspoon sage
1 tablespoon fresh rosemary
1 (28-ounce) can crushed tomatoes
1 (28-ounce) can tomato purée
1 (16-ounce) can white beans,
drained, rinsed
1 cup shell or rotini pasta
Freshly grated Parmesan cheese
Rosemary for garnish

Sauté sausage in 2 tablespoons olive oil in large deep pot for 10 minutes or until slightly browned.

Add carrot, celery, onion, 1 tablespoon rosemary and 1 tablespoon olive oil. Sauté for 5 minutes.

Stir in chicken broth. Add thyme, sage and 1 tablespoon rosemary. Add tomatoes and tomato purée. Bring to a boil; reduce heat. Simmer until heated through.

Stir in beans. Add pasta. Simmer for 20 to 30 minutes or until mixture is heated through and beans and pasta are tender, adding additional chicken broth if desired.

Top each serving with cheese and rosemary garnish.

Yield: 6 servings

SOUPS

Printer's Row was once the center of Midwest publishing.

73

Tortilla Soup

$^1/_2$ cup low-fat reduced-sodium beef
or chicken broth
$1^1/_2$ cups chopped Spanish onions
2 cloves of garlic, crushed
2 cups chopped zucchini
1 large red bell pepper, chopped
1 (10-ounce) package frozen
corn, thawed
2 cups crushed canned Italian
tomatoes, or 6 medium Italian
tomatoes, puréed

$4^1/_2$ cups low-fat reduced-
sodium beef or chicken broth
2 tablespoons chopped cilantro
1 tablespoon hot pepper sauce
1 tablespoon chili powder
Tabasco sauce to taste
4 (6-inch) corn tortillas,
cut into 8 strips
1 cup shredded low-fat
Cheddar cheese

Heat $^1/_2$ cup beef broth in soup pot. Add onions and garlic. Simmer, covered, for 5 minutes.

Add zucchini, red pepper, corn, tomatoes and $4^1/_2$ cups beef broth. Bring to a boil; reduce heat. Simmer for 20 to 25 minutes or until zucchini is tender.

Add cilantro, hot pepper sauce, chili powder and Tabasco sauce.

Spray tortilla strips lightly with nonstick vegetable spray. Place on baking sheet. Bake at 350 degrees for 8 to 10 minutes or until golden brown. Let cool.

Ladle 1 cup hot soup into each soup bowl. Top each serving with 3 to 4 tortilla strips and 2 tablespoons cheese.

Yield: 8 servings

SOUPS

Tomato Soup

3 tablespoons butter or olive oil
1 yellow onion, thinly sliced
1 small carrot, shredded
2 ribs celery, sliced
5 large tomatoes, or 1 large can whole tomatoes
$^1/_2$ cup lightly packed fresh basil
$^3/_4$ teaspoon sugar
$^1/_4$ teaspoon white pepper
$^1/_8$ teaspoon cayenne, or to taste
$1^1/_2$ cups chicken broth
Salt to taste
Fresh basil

Melt butter in large pot. Add onion, carrot and celery. Cook until tender, stirring frequently.

Add tomatoes, basil, sugar, white pepper and cayenne. Bring to a boil, stirring frequently; reduce heat. Simmer, covered, for 10 to 15 minutes or until tomatoes are tender.

At this point, for a smooth soup, purée solids in food processor or blender. Return to pot. For chunkier soup, do not purée.

Add chicken broth and salt. Simmer until heated through. Ladle into soup bowls. Top with fresh basil.

Yield: 1 serving

Hearty Veal and Rice Soup

1 pound veal, chopped or ground
1 onion, chopped
1 cup fresh parsley
3 ribs celery, chopped
3 carrots, chopped
1 cup uncooked rice
1 cup sour cream
Salt and pepper to taste

Brown veal with onion and parsley in large nonstick pot. Add water to cover. Cook until onion and parsley are tender.

Add celery, carrots and rice. Simmer for 2 hours.

Stir in sour cream at serving time. Season with salt and pepper.

Yield: 4 to 6 servings

Curried Salmon Soup

1/4 cup olive oil
1 tablespoon curry powder
2 cups chicken stock
2 cups water
1/2 onion, chopped
1 tablespoon minced ginger
2 cloves of garlic, chopped
1 teaspoon crushed red pepper
1 cup sliced inner bok choy leaves
16 snow peas
1 (16-ounce) salmon fillet, skin removed,
cut into cubes
1/2 cup watercress leaves
1/4 bunch fresh basil, trimmed
1/4 bunch fresh cilantro, trimmed
Salt and black pepper to taste

Heat olive oil in large saucepan over low heat. Add curry powder. Cook for 30 seconds, stirring constantly.

Add chicken stock, water, onion, ginger, garlic and red pepper. Simmer, covered, for 30 minutes.

Strain stock and discard solids. Return stock to saucepan. Add bok choy and snow peas. Simmer, covered, for 3 minutes.

Add salmon. Simmer, covered, for 2 minutes.

Stir in watercress, basil and cilantro. Season with salt and black pepper.

Yield: 4 servings

Oyster Stew

6 tablespoons margarine
1 cup chopped white onion
2 cups chopped peeled potatoes
1 cup chopped celery
1 cup cream
1 1/2 to 2 cups milk
1 teaspoon paprika
Salt and pepper to taste
2 pints shucked oysters
Paprika for garnish

Melt margarine in medium kettle over low heat. Add onion, potatoes and celery. Sauté over low heat just until vegetables begin to soften.

Add cream and milk. Bring to a gentle boil. Add paprika, salt, pepper and undrained oysters. Simmer for 2 minutes.

Ladle into bowls. Garnish with paprika.

Yield: 4 servings

Bay Scallop Chowder

White and tender green
portions of 2 leeks
3 tablespoons unsalted butter
2 ounces thickly sliced smoked
bacon, finely chopped
1 large onion, finely chopped
1 large clove of garlic, minced
$1/2$ teaspoon crushed red pepper
6 cups bottled clam broth
Bouquet garni (2 bay leaves,
5 sprigs of fresh parsley, 3 sprigs of
fresh thyme, 8 black peppercorns)

6 cups chicken stock or
canned low-sodium broth
$1^1/2$ pounds potatoes, peeled,
cut into $1/4$-inch pieces
$2^1/4$ cups whipping cream
2 tablespoons cornstarch
$1^1/2$ pounds bay scallops,
membranes removed
Salt and freshly ground black
pepper to taste
$1/4$ cup finely chopped fresh chives

Cut leeks into halves lengthwise; cut crosswise into $1/8$-inch-thick slices.

Melt butter in large enameled cast-iron pot. Add bacon. Cook over medium-high heat for 2 minutes or until lightly browned.

Add onion. Cook for 7 minutes or until tender, stirring occasionally.

Stir in garlic and red pepper. Cook for 2 minutes or until garlic is fragrant, stirring constantly.

Add clam broth, bouquet garni and chicken stock. Bring to a boil over high heat; reduce heat to medium-high. Simmer for 20 minutes. May be refrigerated for up to 2 days at this point. Bring to a boil before proceeding.

Add potatoes. Cook over medium-high heat for 10 minutes or just until tender. Discard bouquet garni.

Whisk $1/4$ cup of the whipping cream with cornstarch in bowl until smooth. Whisk in remaining 2 cups whipping cream. Whisk into chowder. Bring to a boil. Add leeks. Cook for 4 minutes or just until tender. May let stand at room temperature for up to 3 hours at this point. Rewarm before proceeding.

Stir in scallops. Cook over medium heat for 2 to 3 minutes or until opaque throughout; do not boil. Season with salt and pepper.

Ladle into tureen or individual bowls. Top with chives. Serve immediately.

Yield: 12 servings

SOUPS

NEIGHBO

Lincoln Park

Lincoln Park takes its name from the city's largest park, which flanks this neighborhood. The south end of the park was originally Chicago's first city cemetery. In the 1860s, the graves were removed and plans for a city park were developed. The park itself covers 1,212 acres and is home to the Chicago Historical Society, the Lincoln Park Zoo and the Conservatory.

Lincoln Park serves as the city's year-round playground with access to Lake Michigan and many of Chicago's most popular beaches. Unlike other major American cities, Chicago has preserved almost all of its shoreline as open space for its residents to use and enjoy.

As a place to live, Lincoln Park continues to be one of Chicago's fashionable Lakefront neighborhoods, containing many of the city's notable restaurants and one-of-a-kind specialty shops.

Lagoon in Lincoln Park

Lakefront Picnic

Spring Couscous with Asparagus, Peas and Mint 84

Lamb Burgers with Yogurt Sauce 161

Mediterranean Pasta Salad 89

Sliced Melons

Pine Nut Brown Sugar Shortbread 215

Spring Couscous with Asparagus, Peas and Mint

Salads

Turkey, Black Bean and Orzo Salad, 83

Spring Couscous with Asparagus, Peas and Mint, 84

Coucous Salad, 84

Black Bean, Corn and Tomato Salad, 85

Black Bean and Rice Salad, 85

Chilled Rice Salad, 86

Joe's Pasta Salad, 86

Warm Oriental Chicken Salad, 87

Santa Fe Chicken Salad, 88

Crab Meat Pasta Salad, 88

Mediterranean Pasta Salad, 89

Artichoke Pea Salad, 89

White and Green Salad, 90

Pea and Cashew Salad, 90

Picnic-in-the-Park Potato Salad, 91

Sausage Salad, 91

Five-Spice Chicken Salad in Won Ton Shells, 92

Jicama Chipotle Slaw on Mixed Wild Greens, 93

Jim Saine's and Singapore's Coleslaw, 93

Greek Salad Sandwiches, 94

Country Salad with Goat Cheese and Walnuts, 95

Spiced Pecan Apple Salad, 96

Mandarin Orange Salad, 97

Mango and Green Salad with Baked Goat Cheese, 97

Watercress Salad with Pears and Bleu Cheese, 98

Garlic Salad, 98

Festive Layered Salad, 99

Duck Salad, 99

Crab-Topped Salad Towers, 100

Sherry Wine Vinaigrette, 100

Italian Vinaigrette, 101

Creamy Curry Dressing with Chutney and Ginger, 101

Turkey, Black Bean and Orzo Salad

2 large cloves of garlic, minced
$1/2$ teaspoon salt
3 tablespoons fresh lime juice
$1^1/2$ tablespoons white wine vinegar
1 fresh jalapeño, seeded, chopped
$1^1/2$ teaspoons ground cumin
Salt and pepper to taste
$2/3$ cup olive oil
$1^1/4$ cups orzo (rice-shaped pasta)

8 ounces smoked turkey breast,
cut into bite-size pieces
1 red bell pepper, chopped
1 yellow bell pepper, chopped
$1/2$ red onion, chopped
1 (15-ounce) can black beans,
drained, rinsed
$1/2$ cup finely chopped cilantro
2 avocados, chopped (optional)

Mash garlic with $1/2$ teaspoon salt to make a paste. Combine with lime juice, vinegar, jalapeño, cumin, additional salt and pepper in blender or small food processor container. Add olive oil in a stream with blender running, processing until emulsified.

Cook orzo in boiling salted water in large saucepan until al dente. Drain in colander; rinse with cold water in colander. Let cool. Combine orzo, turkey, bell peppers, onion, beans, cilantro and dressing in large bowl, tossing to mix. Sprinkle avocado over top.

Yield: 6 to 8 servings

SALADS

Spring Couscous with Asparagus, Peas and Mint

5 thin asparagus spears, cut into
thin crossgrain slices
1 (14-ounce) can chicken broth
3/4 cup frozen tiny peas, thawed
1 cup couscous
White part of 1 medium leek, cut into thin
crossgrain slices
1 tablespoon olive oil
1/4 teaspoon salt
Freshly ground pepper to taste
2 tablespoons chopped fresh mint

Steam asparagus in a small amount of water in steamer or saucepan; set aside.

Bring chicken broth to a boil in saucepan. Stir in peas and couscous. Cook until heated through. Remove from heat. Let stand, covered, for 5 minutes.

Add asparagus, leek, olive oil, salt, pepper and mint and mix gently.

Serve warm or at room temperature ladled into soup bowls.

Yield: 4 servings

Couscous Salad

1 1/2 cups boiling chicken broth
1 cup couscous
Chopped parsley to taste
1/4 cup chopped mint
1/4 cup chopped tomato
1/4 cup chopped spring onion
1/4 cup chopped cucumber
1/4 cup chopped red bell pepper
1 tablespoon vegetable oil
3 tablespoons lemon juice

Pour chicken broth over couscous in large bowl. Let stand until cool.

Fluff with fork. Add parsley, mint, tomato, onion, cucumber and red pepper and mix gently. Stir in oil and lemon juice.

Yield: 4 servings

Black Bean, Corn and Tomato Salad

1¹/₂ cups rice, cooked
1 (15-ounce) can black beans, drained, rinsed
1 each orange and red bell pepper, chopped
1 (10-ounce) package frozen corn, thawed
1¹/₂ cups chopped seeded tomatoes
³/₄ cup thinly sliced scallions or green onions
¹/₃ cup fresh cilantro, chopped
¹/₂ cup fresh lemon juice
¹/₄ cup olive oil
¹/₄ cup vegetable oil
2 teaspoons salt
1 tablespoon cumin
1 or 2 dashes of Tabasco sauce

Combine rice, black beans, orange pepper, red pepper, corn, tomatoes, scallions and cilantro in large bowl.

Mix lemon juice, olive oil, vegetable oil, salt, cumin and Tabasco sauce in bowl. Pour over the black bean mixture; mix well.

Chill for 6 hours or longer before serving.

Yield: 4 to 6 servings

Black Bean and Rice Salad

2 (14-ounce) cans chicken broth
¹/₂ cup water
1 (16-ounce) package long grain rice
2 bay leaves
2 (15-ounce) cans black beans, drained, rinsed
1 to 2 red bell peppers, chopped
1 medium red onion, chopped
1 bunch fresh cilantro, chopped
1 tablespoon chili powder
¹/₂ cup olive oil
3 tablespoons orange juice
2 tablespoons red wine vinegar
2 tablespoons ground cumin

Bring chicken broth, water, rice and bay leaves to a boil in saucepan. Simmer until rice is cooked through. Let cool. Remove bay leaves.

Combine rice mixture with beans, red peppers, onion and cilantro in large bowl and mix well.

Mix chili powder, olive oil, orange juice, vinegar and cumin in small bowl. Add to salad and toss well.

Yield: 6 to 8 servings

SALADS

Chilled Rice Salad

$1^1/_2$ tablespoons olive oil
$1^1/_2$ teaspoons curry powder
2 tablespoons chicken base paste
$3^1/_2$ cups water
$1^1/_2$ cups chopped celery
$1^1/_2$ cups rice
$^3/_4$ cup slivered almonds
$^1/_2$ cup mayonnaise
Salt and pepper to taste
Chopped parsley
Cherry tomatoes

Heat olive oil and curry powder in saucepan for 1 minute. Add chicken base, water, celery and rice. Bring to a boil; reduce heat. Simmer, covered, for 20 minutes or until rice is tender. Chill for 6 hours or longer.

Stir in almonds, mayonnaise, salt and pepper. Top with parsley and cherry tomatoes.

Yield: 12 servings

Joe's Pasta Salad

1 pound pasta shells
1 can large black olives, cut into halves lengthwise
2 large red tomatoes, seeded, chopped
1 large yellow tomato, seeded, chopped
1 cup chopped arugula
$^1/_4$ cup chopped fresh basil
1 cup olive oil
$^3/_4$ cup balsamic vinegar
$^1/_2$ cup slivered fresh Parmesan cheese
Salt and pepper to taste
$^1/_4$ cup toasted pine nuts
Fresh basil leaves

Cook pasta al dente using package directions; rinse under cold water and drain.

Toss olives, tomatoes, arugula and chopped basil with pasta in large bowl. Whisk olive oil and vinegar in small bowl. Toss with salad. Add cheese. Season with salt and pepper. Top with pine nuts and basil leaves.

Serve at room temperature.

Yield: 8 to 10 servings

Warm Oriental Chicken Salad

2 cups chicken broth
$^1/_2$ cup soy sauce
$^1/_4$ cup dry sherry
$1^1/_2$ teaspoons Asian chili paste
1 tablespoon oyster sauce
$^1/_4$ cup packed dark brown sugar
2 cloves of garlic, minced
$1^1/_2$ teaspoons finely grated
peeled fresh gingerroot
1 teaspoon ground coriander seeds
1 tablespoon cornstarch
$^1/_4$ cup water

4 whole skinless boneless chicken
breasts, split into halves
1 pound capellini pasta
Salt to taste
3 tablespoons vegetable oil
$^1/_2$ head bok choy, cut into $^1/_4$-inch
slices, or 3 cups
1 red bell pepper, thinly sliced
8 ounces snow peas, trimmed
$^1/_4$ cup each canned bamboo shoots
and water chestnuts, rinsed, drained
$^1/_2$ cup roasted cashews

Whisk chicken broth, soy sauce, sherry, chili paste, oyster sauce, brown sugar, garlic, gingerroot, coriander seeds, cornstarch and water in medium saucepan. Bring to a boil, whisking constantly. Simmer for 5 minutes. Let cool. Reserve 1 cup dressing for marinade. Chill remaining dressing, covered, for 8 to 10 hours.

Rinse chicken and pat dry. Coat with reserved dressing in shallow dish. Chill, covered, for 8 to 10 hours. Drain chicken. Grill on oiled rack 4 inches above glowing coals for 7 minutes per side or until cooked through. Remove and let cool for 10 minutes. Cut into $^1/_4$-inch slices.

Cook pasta al dente in boiling salted water in large kettle; drain well.

Heat wok or large heavy skillet over high heat. Add 2 tablespoons of the oil. Heat until oil begins to smoke. Add bok choy in batches, cooking for 2 minutes per batch or until tender-crisp. Remove to bowl with slotted spoon. Add remaining 1 tablespoon oil to wok. Add bell pepper and snow peas. Stir-fry for 2 minutes or until tender-crisp. Return bok choy to wok. Add bamboo shoots, water chestnuts, cashews and chicken strips and toss well.

Heat remaining dressing in medium saucepan. Toss pasta with chicken mixture and remaining dressing in large bowl.

Asian chili paste and bok choy (Chinese cabbage) are available at Asian markets and at many specialty food shops and supermarkets.

Yield: 8 servings

SALADS

Santa Fe Chicken Salad

4 to 6 chicken breasts, grilled
1 package radiatore pasta
1 bunch cilantro, chopped
Juice of 1 lime
$^1/_2$ cup honey
2 cups frozen corn
2 cups frozen peas
2 large cans black beans, drained
3 zucchini, chopped
1 purple onion, chopped
1 green bell pepper, chopped
1 red bell pepper, chopped
2 tablespoons chili powder, or to taste
2 tablespoons lemon pepper
$^1/_4$ cup cider vinegar
2 tablespoons cumin, or to taste
2 tablespoons cayenne, or to taste

Debone chicken; cut into bite-size pieces. Cook pasta using package directions; drain well.

Combine chicken, pasta, cilantro, lime juice, honey, corn, peas, beans, zucchini, onion, bell peppers, chili powder, lemon pepper, vinegar, cumin and cayenne in large bowl and mix well.

Chill, covered, for 2 to 3 hours.

Yield: 6 to 8 servings

Crab Meat Pasta Salad

1 pound pasta shells
1 can sliced water chestnuts, drained
2 cans crab meat, drained
$^1/_2$ cup freshly grated Parmesan cheese
$^1/_2$ cup sliced red radishes
2 bunches green onions, chopped
1 teaspoon ground red pepper
1 tablespoon black pepper
1 cup ranch salad dressing

Cook pasta al dente using package directions; drain.

Combine with water chestnuts, crab meat, cheese, radishes, green onions, red pepper and black pepper in large bowl and mix well. Toss with salad dressing.

Chill, covered, for 6 hours or longer.

Yield: 8 to 10 servings

Mediterranean Pasta Salad

1 pound pasta shells
$1^1/_2$ cups olive oil
$^1/_2$ cup lemon juice
10 ounces shrimp, cooked, peeled
1 pound feta cheese, cut into $^1/_2$-inch cubes
3 medium tomatoes, seeded, chopped
$^1/_2$ cup chopped chives or scallions
2 teaspoons chopped fresh or dried oregano
2 cloves of garlic, chopped
Greek olives
Artichoke hearts

Cook pasta using package directions; drain well. Toss with oil and lemon juice in large bowl. Add shrimp, cheese, tomatoes, chives, oregano and garlic and mix well. Top with olives and artichoke hearts.
Chill, covered, for 1 hour.

Yield: 8 to 10 servings

Artichoke Pea Salad

1 (10-ounce) package frozen peas
with mushrooms
2 hard-cooked eggs, chopped
$^1/_4$ cup sweet pickle relish
2 tablespoons chopped onion
$1^1/_2$ cups mayonnaise
2 tablespoons lemon juice
1 teaspoon salt
$^1/_2$ teaspoon pepper
$^1/_2$ teaspoon dill
$^1/_4$ teaspoon oregano
$^1/_4$ teaspoon dry mustard
4 artichokes, cooked, chilled, chokes removed
Pimento strips

Cook peas using package directions; drain. Mix with eggs, relish and onion in large bowl.
Mix mayonnaise, lemon juice, salt, pepper, dill, oregano and dry mustard in small bowl. Stir approximately $^1/_2$ cup into egg mixture to moisten. Spoon into artichokes. Chill artichokes and remaining mayonnaise mixture until serving time.
Top with pimento strips. Serve with remaining mayonnaise mixture.

Yield: 4 servings

SALADS

White and Green Salad

3 ribs celery
$^1/_2$ cup salad oil
3 tablespoons lemon juice
3 tablespoons tarragon vinegar
2 tablespoons sugar
1 teaspoon minced onion
$^1/_2$ teaspoon oregano
1 teaspoon salt
$^1/_8$ teaspoon pepper, or to taste
1 (8-ounce) can hearts of palm, cut into sections
1 (8-ounce) can white asparagus,
cut into sections
1 (8-ounce) can celery hearts, chopped
1 avocado, chopped
1 head Boston lettuce

Clean celery; cut off tops and bottoms and discard. Chop remaining celery finely in food processor or blender. Add oil, lemon juice, vinegar, sugar, onion, oregano, salt and pepper and blend well.

Combine hearts of palm, asparagus, celery hearts and avocado in large bowl. Pour dressing over salad. Marinate in refrigerator for several hours.

Serve over lettuce leaves.

Yield: 6 servings

Pea and Cashew Salad

1 (10-ounce) package frozen fresh peas,
lightly cooked, chilled
1 cup coarsely chopped cashews
6 slices bacon, crisp-fried, crumbled
$^1/_2$ cup chopped celery
$^1/_4$ cup chopped sweet onion
$^1/_2$ cup sour cream
$^1/_2$ teaspoon salt

Combine peas, cashews, bacon, celery, onion, sour cream and salt in large bowl and mix well. Chill for 4 hours or longer.

Yield: 6 servings

Picnic-in-the-Park Potato Salad

2$^1/_2$ pounds red potatoes
$^1/_2$ cup toasted pine nuts
1 green apple, chopped
1 medium red onion, chopped
1 cup raisins
3 tablespoons fennel seeds
$^1/_2$ cup balsamic vinegar
$^1/_4$ cup olive oil
Salt and pepper to taste

Cook potatoes in boiling water in large pot for 12 minutes or just until tender; drain. Let cool. Cut into 1-inch pieces.

Combine potatoes, pine nuts, apple, onion, raisins and fennel seeds in large bowl and mix well. Toss with vinegar and olive oil. Season with salt and pepper.

Chill thoroughly.

Yield: 6 to 8 servings

Sausage Salad

1 pound string beans, trimmed
Salt to taste
8 ounces Gruyère cheese, cut into bite-size cubes
4 ounces Genoa salami, cut into $^1/_2$-inch strips
1 recipe Sherry Wine Vinaigrette (page 100)

Cook beans in boiling salted water in large saucepan just until tender. Rinse under cold water and drain.

Combine beans, cheese and salami in large bowl and mix well. Toss with Sherry Wine Vinaigrette.

Yield: 4 servings

Five-Spice Chicken Salad in Won Ton Shells

48 frozen won ton wrappers,
thawed
2 teaspoons five-spice powder
1^1/$_2$ teaspoons salt
1 large whole skinless boneless
chicken breast

1 medium navel orange
1 large shallot, minced
1 tablespoon rice wine vinegar
1 tablespoon honey
1 tablespoon olive oil
^{1}/$_2$ cup finely chopped fresh cilantro

Trim won ton wrappers to form 2-inch squares. Coat nonstick miniature muffin cups with butter-flavored cooking spray. Press 1 square into each muffin cup. Coat squares lightly with cooking spray. Bake at 350 degrees for 7 minutes or until lightly browned. Cool in pan. Repeat process until all won ton wrappers are baked. Won ton shells may be stored in airtight container at room temperature for up to 1 week.

Mix five-spice powder and salt in small bowl. Rinse chicken and pat dry. Sprinkle chicken with spice mixture. Place chicken on lightly oiled baking sheet. Bake at 350 degrees for 18 minutes or until cooked through. Let cool and cut into ^{1}/$_4$-inch cubes.

Remove zest from half the orange with vegetable peeler. Cut zest into very thin 1-inch strips. Reserve 1 packed teaspoon of zest; discard remainder or reserve for another use. Peel orange with sharp knife, removing all the white pith. Hold orange over bowl and cut with sharp knife between membranes to release sections. Chop sections into ^{1}/$_4$-inch pieces. Reserve 1 table-spoon of the released orange juice.

Combine orange pieces, shallot, reserved orange juice, vinegar, honey and olive oil in medium bowl. Add chicken, half the orange zest and half the cilantro and stir gently.

Spoon 2 teaspoons chicken salad into each won ton shell. Top with remaining orange zest and cilantro.

Won ton wrappers are available in the produce department or freezer section of most supermarkets. Five-spice powder is available at Asian markets.

Yield: 4 dozen

SALADS

Jicama Chipotle Slaw on Mixed Wild Greens

1 large jicama, peeled, chopped
1 red bell pepper, cut into $^1/_4$-inch pieces
$^1/_2$ bunch green onions, chopped
$^1/_2$ cup cooked black beans, rinsed
$^1/_2$ cup roasted corn
1 small Spanish onion, chopped
$1^1/_2$ tablespoons chipotle paste
$^1/_3$ cup extra-virgin olive oil
$^1/_4$ cup rice wine or Champagne vinegar
$1^1/_2$ teaspoons kosher salt
$1^1/_2$ teaspoons minced garlic
4 ounces mixed young wild greens
Chopped cilantro to taste

Combine jicama, bell pepper, green onions, beans, corn, Spanish onion, chipotle paste, olive oil, vinegar, salt and garlic in large nonreactive bowl and mix well. Chill for 1 hour or longer.

Serve over mixed greens. Top with cilantro.

Yield: 4 servings

Jim Saine's and Singapore's Coleslaw

The following recipe is the most famous coleslaw Chicago has ever known. It was created by restaurateur Bill Simmons when he operated a popular place in Chicago named The Pit. Later, two great Rush Street restaurants, The Singapore and Jim Saine's, obtained it from Simmons and competed with each other for the recognition of making it famous. Hollywood, New York, and other out-of-town hosts would send for it by plane. A few years ago, Jack Brickhouse saw Bill Simmons at Binyon's Restaurant, and, while they were reminiscing about the "good old days" on Rush Street, Bill promised to send Jack his famous recipe. Bill kept his promise, and now we are sending it along to you.

$2^1/_2$ pounds cabbage, shredded
1 teaspoon salt or salt substitute
$^1/_4$ teaspoon white pepper
$1^1/_2$ cups sugar or equivalent artificial sweetener
2 tablespoons cider vinegar
$^1/_2$ cup mayonnaise or light mayonnaise
2 cups sour cream or sour half-and-half

Combine cabbage, salt, pepper, sugar, vinegar, mayonnaise and sour cream in large bowl and mix well. Chill, covered, for 12 hours or longer.

Will keep in refrigerator for 2 to 3 days; drain partially after first day.

Yield: 4 to 6 servings

Greek Salad Sandwiches

12 ounces small tomatoes, cored,
cut into halves, thinly sliced
6 cups small spinach leaves,
stems trimmed
$1^1/_2$ cups thinly sliced English
hothouse cucumber
1 cup crumbled feta cheese
$^1/_3$ cup coarsely chopped kalamata
or other pitted black
brine-cured olives

16 large fresh basil leaves,
thinly sliced
$^1/_4$ cup olive oil
5 teaspoons fresh lemon juice
1 large clove of garlic, minced
Salt and pepper to taste
4 (5- to 6-inch) pita bread
rounds, toasted

Drain tomatoes in a strainer for 15 minutes.

Combine tomatoes, spinach, cucumber, cheese, olives and basil in large bowl and mix gently.

Combine olive oil, lemon juice and garlic in small bowl. Whisk until blended. Season with salt and pepper.

Pour dressing over salad, tossing to coat.

Cut pita rounds into halves crosswise.

Divide salad mixture among 8 pita halves.

Yield: 4 servings

SALADS

94

Country Salad with Goat Cheese and Walnuts

3/4 cup walnut oil	1/8 teaspoon toasted cumin seeds,
2 to 2 1/4 ounces aged sherry vinegar	or to taste
Salt and pepper to taste	2 to 3 apples
Tabasco sauce to taste	10 to 12 cups mixed baby lettuces,
1/4 cup boiling water	rinsed, trimmed
1 large shallot, minced	1 cup toasted walnuts
1 tablespoon unsalted butter	1 cup toasted croutons
1 cup whipping cream	8 goat cheese buttons
6 ounces soft goat cheese	1 tablespoon minced chives

For vinaigrette, combine walnut oil, vinegar, salt, pepper and Tabasco sauce in blender container. Add boiling water in a stream with blender running, processing until emulsified. Let cool. Store in refrigerator for up to 2 days.

For fondue, cook shallot in butter in saucepan until wilted. Add whipping cream. Bring to a boil. Whisk in goat cheese until smooth. Stir in cumin seeds. Season to taste. Let cool. Store in refrigerator for up to 2 days. Reheat in double boiler over hot water.

Slice apples into 24 chips. Toss greens, walnuts and croutons with 1 cup of the vinaigrette in large bowl.

Arrange salad on 1 side of each plate. Place goat cheese button on other side. Top cheese with a small amount of fondue. Top with apple chips and chives.

Yield: 8 servings

SALADS

Spiced Pecan Apple Salad

3 tablespoons butter
1 teaspoon salt
1 teaspoon ground cinnamon
$^1/_4$ teaspoon cayenne
$1^2/_3$ cups pecan pieces
1 large Red Delicious apple
2 teaspoons (about) lemon juice
1 head Boston lettuce, chilled, torn
into bite-size pieces

1 head red leaf lettuce, chilled, torn
into bite-size pieces
8 ounces feta cheese, crumbled
2 tablespoons sherry wine vinegar
1 tablespoon Dijon mustard
$^1/_2$ cup extra-light olive oil

Place butter on baking sheet with sides. Heat in 350-degree oven until melted.

Stir in salt, cinnamon and cayenne. Sprinkle evenly with pecans, stirring with rubber spatula to coat pecans. Bake for 15 minutes or until pecans are aromatic and golden brown. Cool on baking sheet on wire rack.

Cut apple into $^1/_4$-inch pieces and sprinkle with lemon juice.

Combine lettuce, apple and cheese in large bowl.

Whisk vinegar and Dijon mustard in small bowl. Whisk in olive oil gradually until thickened.

Drizzle over salad. Top with spiced pecans.

Yield: 8 servings

SALADS

Mandarin Orange Salad

$^{1}/_{2}$ teaspoon salt
$^{1}/_{8}$ teaspoon pepper, or to taste
2 tablespoons sugar
2 tablespoons vinegar
$^{1}/_{4}$ cup salad oil
4 drops of Tabasco sauce
1 tablespoon snipped parsley
$^{1}/_{4}$ cup sliced almonds
4 teaspoons sugar
$^{1}/_{2}$ head lettuce, torn into bite-size pieces
$^{1}/_{2}$ bunch romaine, torn into bite-size pieces
$^{3}/_{4}$ cup chopped celery
2 green onions, thinly sliced
1 (11-ounce) can mandarin oranges, drained

Combine salt, pepper, 2 tablespoons sugar, vinegar, oil, Tabasco sauce and parsley in jar; cover tightly and shake well. Chill until needed.

Cook almonds and 4 teaspoons sugar in saucepan over low heat until sugar is dissolved and almonds are coated, stirring constantly. Let cool; break apart. Store at room temperature.

Place lettuces in sealable plastic bag. Add celery and green onions. Seal and chill until needed.

Pour dressing into the plastic bag. Add mandarin oranges. Seal bag and shake until greens and oranges are coated. Add almonds and shake again or sprinkle over salads if serving on individual plates.

Yield: 6 servings

Mango and Green Salad with Baked Goat Cheese

1 cup bread crumbs
2 tablespoons basil-flavored oil
Salt and pepper to taste
8 ounces goat cheese
2 tablespoons fruit-flavored vinegar
1 shallot, minced
$^{1}/_{4}$ cup basil-flavored oil
$1^{1}/_{2}$ quarts mixed greens, torn into
bite-size pieces
1 mango, peeled, sliced

Toss bread crumbs with 2 tablespoons oil, salt and pepper in bowl. Place in heated sauté pan. Sauté over medium heat until lightly browned. Set aside to cool.

Cut cheese into eight 1-ounce pieces; shape pieces into $^{1}/_{2}$-inch-thick rounds. Press the rounds into the bread crumbs to coat well. Place on baking sheet. Warm in 350-degree oven for 5 minutes.

Combine vinegar and shallot in stainless steel bowl. Add $^{1}/_{4}$ cup oil gradually, whisking constantly. Season to taste.

Toss greens with some of the vinaigrette in large bowl. Divide among 4 plates. Divide mango among 4 plates. Place 2 rounds of cheese on each plate. Drizzle with remaining vinaigrette.

Yield: 4 servings

SALADS

Watercress Salad with Pears and Bleu Cheese

2 tablespoons raspberry vinegar
Juice of $1/2$ lemon
$1/2$ cup olive oil
2 tablespoons whipping cream
Salt and pepper to taste
2 bunches watercress, rinsed, stems removed
$1/2$ cup crumbled bleu cheese
2 Bosc pears, thinly sliced

Mix vinegar, lemon juice, olive oil, whipping cream, salt and pepper in bowl.
Toss with watercress, cheese and pears.
Serve immediately.

Yield: 6 servings

Garlic Salad

2 tablespoons butter
1 clove of garlic, minced
4 English muffin halves, cut into cubes
Juice of 1 lemon
3 cloves of garlic, minced
$3/4$ cup olive oil
Salt and pepper to taste
2 heads romaine lettuce, torn into bite-size pieces
1 cup Swiss cheese, cut into thin strips
8 ounces bacon, crisp-fried, crumbled
2 cups cherry tomato halves
$2/3$ cup pine nuts
$1/3$ cup grated Parmesan cheese

Melt butter in skillet over medium heat. Add 1 garlic clove. Sauté briefly. Add bread cubes. Cook until golden brown.
Mix lemon juice, 3 garlic cloves and olive oil in medium bowl. Season with salt and pepper.
Toss lettuce, Swiss cheese, bacon, tomatoes, pine nuts and Parmesan cheese in large bowl. Toss with dressing. Stir in croutons.

Yield: 8 servings

SALADS

Festive Layered Salad

1 large bunch romaine lettuce, shredded into
bite-size pieces
1 cup sliced mushrooms
1 medium red onion, thinly sliced
1 cup sliced Swiss cheese, cut into bite-size
pieces
1 quart fresh strawberries, sliced
$^1/_2$ cup toasted crushed walnuts

Layer lettuce, mushrooms, onion, cheese and
strawberries in trifle bowl or other deep glass bowl.
Sprinkle with walnuts.
Serve with a poppyseed salad dressing.

Yield: 6 servings

Duck Salad

$^1/_2$ teaspoon dry mustard
3 tablespoons lemon juice
$^1/_4$ teaspoon salt
Pepper to taste
6 tablespoons olive oil
3 cups julienned roast duck
1 small Bermuda onion, thinly sliced
Grated peel of 1 orange
1 tablespoon butter
$^1/_4$ teaspoon garlic salt
$^1/_4$ cup coarsely chopped walnuts
3 medium oranges, peeled, thinly sliced
Lettuce leaves

Combine dry mustard, lemon juice, salt and
pepper in blender container. Add olive oil in a stream
with blender running, processing until emulsified.
Combine duck and onion in large bowl. Add $^1/_2$
cup of the dressing and orange peel and toss. Chill,
covered, for 2 hours.
Heat butter in skillet over medium heat. Add
garlic salt and walnuts. Sauté until golden brown.
Add orange slices to duck mixture and toss gently.
Serve over bed of lettuce. Sprinkle with walnut
mixture.

Yield: 4 servings

SALADS

Crab-Topped Salad Towers

2 cups mayonnaise
1 green bell pepper, finely chopped
$^1/_4$ cup finely chopped onion
$^1/_4$ cup chili sauce
2 tablespoons catsup
2 teaspoons Worcestershire sauce
Salt and paprika to taste
1 (7-ounce) can crab meat, flaked
2 hard-boiled eggs, chopped
2 to 3 large bunches watercress or chopped
lettuce
8 pieces of toast, crusts trimmed
2 avocados, cut into 8 slices
8 tomato slices
8 deviled egg halves, sliced

Combine mayonnaise, green pepper, onion, chili sauce, catsup, Worcestershire sauce, salt and paprika in large bowl and mix well. Fold in crab meat and hard-boiled eggs. Cover and chill thoroughly.
Place 1 mound of watercress on each of 8 luncheon plates. Add toast, avocado slices, tomato slices and deviled eggs. Top with crab dressing.

Yield: 8 servings

Sherry Wine Vinaigrette

3 tablespoons Dijon mustard
$^1/_3$ cup sherry wine vinegar
Salt and pepper to taste
$^3/_4$ cup vegetable oil

Combine Dijon mustard, vinegar, salt and pepper in food processor container. Add oil in a stream with food processor running, processing until emulsified.

Yield: 1 to $1^1/_4$ cups

Italian Vinaigrette

$^{1}/_{3}$ cup cider vinegar or balsamic vinegar
$^{2}/_{3}$ cup salad oil
2 teaspoons sugar or equivalent
artificial sweetener
1 teaspoon salt
$^{1}/_{2}$ teaspoon pepper
2 whole cloves of garlic
1 teaspoon parsley flakes

Combine vinegar, oil, sugar, salt, pepper, garlic and parsley flakes in bottle or jar; cover and shake well. Store in refrigerator.

Yield: 1 cup

Creamy Curry Dressing with Chutney and Ginger

1 tablespoon vegetable oil
2 tablespoons minced fresh gingerroot
1 teaspoon minced fresh garlic
$^{1}/_{4}$ cup minced green onions
1 cup whipping cream
$^{1}/_{4}$ teaspoon curry powder
2 tablespoons chutney
$^{1}/_{8}$ teaspoon salt
$^{1}/_{8}$ teaspoon cayenne
$2^{1}/_{2}$ tablespoons plain yogurt
2 tablespoons minced parsley

Heat oil in large skillet. Add gingerroot, garlic and green onions. Sauté for $1^{1}/_{2}$ minutes or until tender.
Stir in whipping cream gradually. Simmer until liquid is reduced enough to lightly coat a spoon. Stir in curry powder. Simmer for 1 minute. Stir in chutney, salt and cayenne. Remove from heat. Stir in yogurt and parsley.
Makes excellent dressing for crisp salad greens.

Yield: $1^{1}/_{2}$ cups

Little Italy

Of all the immigrants to Chicago's Near West Side in the late 1800s, the Italians stayed the longest. Little Italy remains Chicago's oldest continuously Italian neighborhood. Taylor Street is the heart of Little Italy. During Prohibition, Taylor Street was the scene of many gun battles, but today some of the area's best-known stores and Italian restaurants are found here. Lining the street are rehabbed brick and frame houses built by young, local residents and professionals attracted to the area by the West Side Medical Center and the University of Illinois Chicago campus. Also on the University grounds is Hull House, a museum of Jane Addams' original settlement house that was founded in 1889.

A lemonade stand in Chicago's Little Italy neighborhood

Taylor Street Supper

Bruschetta 18

Shrimp and Vegetable Pasta 109

Garlic Salad 98

Italian Bread

Tiramisù 224

Shrimp and Vegetable Pasta

Pasta, Grains & Rice

Cheese Ravioli with Smoked Tomato Sauce

4 medium tomatoes, cut into halves
$^1/_4$ small onion
1 cup Merlot
2 teaspoons olive oil
1 teaspoon liquid smoke
1 clove of garlic, chopped

Oregano to taste
Basil to taste
Salt and white pepper to taste
1 pound fresh or frozen
cheese ravioli
Grated Parmesan cheese

Combine tomatoes and onion with enough water to cover in saucepan. Bring to a boil.

Boil for 5 minutes; drain. Combine tomatoes, onion, Merlot, olive oil, liquid smoke, garlic, oregano and basil in blender container.

Process at low speed for 10 seconds or until coarsely chopped. Pour into saucepan.

Simmer for 30 minutes, stirring occasionally. Season with salt and white pepper.

Cook ravioli using package directions; drain. Transfer to serving platter or pasta bowl. Top with the tomato mixture; sprinkle with Parmesan cheese.

Yield: 4 servings

Lemon Orzo

5 cups chicken broth, skimmed
2 cups orzo
$1/4$ cup minced fresh chives
2 teaspoons finely grated lemon zest
2 teaspoons peanut oil
2 teaspoons fresh lemon juice

Bring broth to a boil in saucepan; reduce heat. Stir in orzo.

Simmer for 5 minutes or until tender; drain.

Return pasta to saucepan. Add chives, lemon zest, peanut oil and lemon juice, mixing until combined. Serve immediately.

Great served with chicken or salmon.

Yield: 4 to 6 servings

Pasta with Marinated Tomatoes

2 large tomatoes, seeded, coarsely chopped
10 to 12 oil-pack sun-dried tomatoes, drained, coarsely chopped
$1/4$ cup extra-virgin olive oil
1 to 2 cloves of garlic, chopped
Salt and freshly ground pepper to taste
8 to 12 ounces penne or fusilli
$3/4$ cup loosely packed fresh basil leaves

Combine tomatoes, olive oil, garlic, salt and pepper in bowl and mix well.

Marinate at room temperature for 45 minutes, stirring occasionally.

Cook pasta in enough water to cover in saucepan for 7 to 10 minutes or until al dente; drain.

Combine hot pasta and tomato mixture in bowl, tossing to mix. Stir in basil.

Serve warm or at room temperature.

Yield: 4 to 6 servings

Shrimp and Vegetable Pasta

4 slices bacon
1 cup chopped onion
1 medium green bell pepper, chopped
4 carrots, sliced diagonally
$^1/_4$ teaspoon garlic powder
2 (14-ounce) cans whole tomatoes, chopped
1 (2-ounce) can sliced ripe olives, drained
1 teaspoon dried basil
1 teaspoon dried oregano
$^1/_4$ teaspoon pepper
$^1/_4$ teaspoon garlic salt
1 pound medium shrimp, peeled and deveined
8 ounces fresh mushrooms, sliced
$^1/_4$ cup red wine
1 (16-ounce) package pasta, cooked, drained
Grated Parmesan cheese

Cook bacon in large skillet until crisp; remove bacon and pat dry. Crumble bacon and reserve for topping.

Sauté onion, green pepper, carrots and garlic powder in 1 tablespoon bacon drippings in skillet until carrots are tender-crisp.

Add undrained tomatoes, olives, basil, oregano, pepper and garlic salt. Bring to a boil. Cover and reduce heat. Cook for 3 to 5 minutes or until olives are heated through. Add shrimp, mushrooms and wine. Cook for 10 minutes, stirring frequently.

Serve over pasta. Sprinkle with bacon bits and cheese and serve immediately.

Yield: 6 servings

Linguini with Onion Confit and Goat Cheese

1 tablespoon olive oil
4 cups thinly sliced yellow onions
$^1/_2$ teaspoon salt
2 cloves of garlic, minced
$^1/_4$ cup white wine
9 ounces fresh linguini
$^1/_3$ cup chopped fresh basil
3 tablespoons chopped walnuts, toasted
1 ounce goat cheese, crumbled
Pepper to taste

Heat olive oil in skillet over medium heat until hot. Stir in onions and salt.

Cook, covered, for 15 minutes, stirring occasionally. Stir in garlic.

Cook, uncovered, for 15 minutes or until golden brown, stirring frequently. Add wine and mix well.

Simmer for 3 minutes, stirring occasionally. Remove from heat. Cover to keep warm.

Cook pasta using package directions. Drain, reserving $^1/_4$ cup cooking liquid.

Combine reserved cooking liquid, pasta, basil, walnuts, goat cheese and pepper with onion confit in bowl and mix well.

Serve immediately.

Yield: 5 servings

Penne with Vodka and Tomato Cream Sauce

1 tablespoon butter	$^1/_4$ cup vodka
1 tablespoon olive oil	$^1/_4$ cup crushed red pepper
1 onion, chopped	Salt and black pepper to taste
1 (28-ounce) can chopped	1 pound penne
plum tomatoes	Freshly grated Parmesan cheese
1 cup whipping cream	Chopped fresh chives

Heat butter and olive oil in saucepan over medium heat until butter melts. Add onion. Sauté for 8 minutes or until tender. Add tomatoes and mix well.

Cook for 25 minutes or until most of the liquid is absorbed, stirring frequently. Stir in whipping cream, vodka and red pepper. Bring to a boil.

Boil for 2 minutes or until thickened and of sauce consistency, stirring constantly. Season with salt and black pepper. Remove from heat. Cover to keep warm.

Cook pasta using package directions until al dente; drain. Transfer to a serving bowl. Pour sauce over pasta, tossing to mix. Sprinkle with cheese and chives. Serve immediately.

May prepare sauce 1 day in advance and store, covered, in refrigerator.

Yield: 4 servings

PASTA, GRAINS & RICE

Sun-Dried Tomato and Spinach Penne

8 cloves of garlic, crushed
$^1/_4$ cup olive oil
1 (10-ounce) package frozen cut spinach,
thawed, drained
1 teaspoon oregano
$^1/_2$ teaspoon basil
$^1/_2$ teaspoon salt
$^1/_4$ teaspoon black pepper
$^1/_4$ teaspoon red pepper flakes
$^1/_2$ cup chopped oil-pack sun-dried tomatoes
1 cup imported grated Romano cheese
$1^1/_2$ pounds penne, cooked, drained

Sauté garlic in olive oil in skillet until light brown. Stir in spinach, oregano, basil, salt, black pepper and red pepper flakes.

Cook over low heat for 15 minutes, stirring frequently. Stir in tomatoes and cheese.

Cook for 10 minutes, stirring frequently. Spoon over pasta in bowl, tossing to mix.

Yield: 6 servings

Chicken Vegetable Lasagna

1 package lasagna noodles
1 pound boneless skinless chicken breasts,
cut into cubes
$^1/_2$ red onion, chopped
$^1/_4$ cup butter
3 large carrots, sliced
1 cup frozen or fresh peas
3 tablespoons flour
1 teaspoon each basil, thyme and sage
1 cup chicken stock
2 cups whipping cream
Salt and pepper to taste
1 (16-ounce) can stewed whole Italian tomatoes,
drained, cut into halves
1 cup mozzarella cheese

Cook lasagna using package directions; drain well. Rinse chicken and pat dry.

Sauté onion in butter in skillet for 2 minutes. Add carrots and peas. Sauté for 2 minutes or until tender. Add flour. Cook over low heat for 1 minute, stirring constantly. Add basil, thyme and sage. Stir in chicken stock and whipping cream gradually. Bring to a boil. Boil for 1 minute, stirring constantly. Add chicken. Cook for 5 minutes. Season with salt and pepper.

Spoon a layer of the chicken mixture over the bottom of a 10x12-inch glass baking dish. Add the lasagna, remaining chicken mixture, tomatoes and cheese one-half at a time. Bake at 375 degrees for 40 minutes. Broil for 5 minutes or until browned. Let stand for 5 to 10 minutes before serving.

Yield: 4 to 6 servings

Pasta Puntanesca

2 Spanish onions, thickly sliced,
separated into rings
6 cloves of garlic, crushed
4 to 6 tablespoons butter
4 jalapeños, sliced
1 habañero pepper, sliced
4 (28-ounce) cans crushed tomatoes
3 to 4 (26-ounce) jars Classico Spicy
Red Pepper Sauce
3 green bell peppers, sliced
2 red bell peppers, sliced
6 to 12 tomatoes, sliced,
cut into quarters
Oregano to taste

Basil to taste
Italian seasoning to taste
2 cloves of garlic, sliced
1 dried red pepper
Salt and black pepper to taste
2 (4-ounce) packages Italian
sausage, grilled,
cut into bite-size pieces
1 pound rigatoni or fusilli
3 to 4 tablespoons olive oil
2 to 3 tablespoons butter
2 (8-ounce) cans pitted black
olives, drained
1 cup chopped fresh basil

Sauté onions and crushed garlic in 4 to 6 tablespoons butter in stockpot until onions are light brown. Stir in jalapeños and habañero. Add crushed tomatoes, Spicy Red Pepper Sauce, bell peppers, sliced tomatoes, oregano, basil and Italian seasoning and mix well.

Cook on high for 15 minutes, stirring frequently. Add sliced garlic. Snip dried red pepper with kitchen shears into stockpot.

Cook on low until thickened, stirring occasionally. Season with salt and black pepper. Add sausage and mix well.

Simmer over low heat for 20 to 30 minutes, stirring frequently.

Cook pasta using package directions, adding salt and olive oil to water; drain. Combine pasta with 2 to 3 tablespoons butter, tossing until mixed. Transfer to a serving platter. Spoon sauce over pasta. Top with olives and chopped fresh basil.

Yield: 8 to 10 servings

PASTA, GRAINS & RICE

Angel Hair Pasta with Three Caviars

8 ounces angel hair pasta
4 quarts boiling water
2 tablespoons vegetable oil
$^1/_3$ cup minced fresh chives
2 hard-boiled egg yolks, finely chopped
$^1/_4$ cup sour cream
2 tablespoons freshly squeezed lemon juice
$^3/_4$ cup whipping cream
6 tablespoons (or more) golden caviar
6 tablespoons (or more) red caviar
6 tablespoons (or more) black caviar

Chill servings plates.

Cook pasta in boiling water in large pot until al dente; drain and rinse in cold water. Drain again. Place in large bowl and toss with oil.

Mix most of the chives and most of the egg yolks gently in small bowl, reserving a small amount of each for topping.

Blend sour cream, lemon juice and whipping cream in large bowl just before serving time. Mix gently with pasta. Stir in mixture of chives and egg yolks; do not refrigerate.

Arrange pasta on chilled plates. Spoon dollops of each caviar over each serving. Top with reserved chives and egg yolks.

Yield: 4 servings

Red Clam Linguini

16 ounces linguini
6 quarts water
1 to 2 tablespoons olive oil
Salt to taste
4 cloves of garlic, chopped
$^1/_4$ cup olive oil
1 teaspoon crushed red pepper
$^1/_2$ teaspoon oregano
$^1/_2$ teaspoon basil
1 (16-ounce) can crushed tomatoes
1 bottle clam juice
2 Roma tomatoes, seeded, chopped
3 (6-ounce) cans chopped clams, undrained
2 tablespoons chopped fresh parsley
2 tablespoons fresh lemon juice
Black pepper to taste
Grated Romano cheese

Cook linguini in water with 1 to 2 tablespoons olive oil and salt in large pot until al dente; drain. Cover to keep warm.

Sauté garlic in $^1/_4$ cup olive oil in saucepan over low heat for 30 seconds. Add red pepper, oregano and basil. Stir in canned tomatoes, clam juice, Roma tomatoes and undrained clams.

Simmer for 5 minutes, stirring occasionally. Add parsley, lemon juice, salt and black pepper and mix well. Pour over hot linguini on serving platter. Sprinkle with Romano cheese.

Yield: 4 servings

PASTA, GRAINS & RICE

Fettuccini with Scallops, Citrus and Herbs

12 ounces asparagus
1 cup white wine
1 clove of garlic, crushed
1 pound bay scallops or shrimp
1 cup cream
$^1/_2$ cup sliced scallions and tops
1 tablespoon chopped fresh
tarragon, or
1 teaspoon dried tarragon

$^3/_4$ teaspoon grated orange peel
$^1/_2$ teaspoon grated lemon peel
$^3/_4$ teaspoon salt
$^1/_4$ teaspoon pepper
1 pound fettuccini
Salt to taste
2 tablespoons butter,
cut into 4 pieces
Sprigs of fresh tarragon

Cut asparagus stems into $^1/_2$-inch pieces; cut tips to $1^1/_2$-inch lengths.

Combine wine and garlic in saucepan. Bring to a simmer. Add scallops.

Simmer for 30 seconds or until tender. Remove scallops to bowl with slotted spoon.

Cook remaining wine mixture over medium-high heat for 7 minutes or until liquid is reduced to $^1/_2$ cup. Discard garlic clove. Stir in cream.

Cook over medium heat for 5 minutes or until slightly thickened, stirring constantly. Stir in scallions, tarragon, orange peel, lemon peel, salt and pepper. Add scallops and mix well. Remove from heat.

Cook fettuccini in boiling salted water in stockpot for 6 minutes. Add asparagus.

Cook for 3 minutes longer or until pasta is al dente and asparagus is tender-crisp; drain.

Transfer pasta and asparagus to heated serving platter or divide among individual dinner plates.

Reheat scallop mixture over low heat, stirring occasionally. Stir in butter 1 piece at a time. Spoon over pasta mixture. Top with tarragon sprigs.

Yield: 6 servings

PASTA, GRAINS & RICE

The Hull House mansion on the University of Illinois grounds

Fra Diablo

6 cloves of garlic, chopped
3 tablespoons olive oil
1 cup dry white wine
Juice of 1 lemon
1 (16-ounce) can crushed tomatoes
1 teaspoon dried thyme
2 teaspoons crushed red pepper
2 large Roma tomatoes, chopped
$^1/_4$ cup fresh basil, chopped
1 pound large shrimp, peeled
Salt and black pepper to taste
1 package linguini, cooked, drained
Grated Romano cheese

Sauté garlic in olive oil in large kettle until garlic begins to sizzle.

Add wine. Boil until liquid is reduced to $^1/_4$ cup.

Add lemon juice, crushed tomatoes, thyme and red pepper. Simmer over low heat for 20 minutes.

Add Roma tomatoes, basil and shrimp. Simmer for 5 to 7 minutes or just until shrimp turn pink. Season with salt and black pepper.

Serve over linguini. Sprinkle with cheese.

Yield: 3 servings

Greek Tuna Pasta

2 large tomatoes
$^1/_4$ cup olive oil
6 cloves of garlic, chopped
2 tablespoons capers, drained
$^1/_2$ cup sliced kalamata olives
2 tablespoons red wine vinegar
1 tablespoon balsamic vinegar
1 teaspoon crushed red pepper
$^3/_4$ cup crumbled feta cheese
1 small bunch fresh spinach, stems removed
1 pound fresh tuna, cut into 1-inch chunks
Salt and black pepper to taste
1 package spaghettini, cooked, drained
Grated Romano cheese

Blanch tomatoes in boiling water in saucepan. Remove when skin begins to blister and let cool. Remove and discard skin and seeds.

Heat olive oil in large saucepan over low heat. Add garlic. Sauté for 30 seconds.

Add tomatoes, capers, olives and vinegar. Simmer for 10 minutes.

Add red pepper, feta cheese and spinach. Cook for 30 seconds, stirring constantly.

Add tuna. Simmer for 3 to 4 minutes over medium-high heat or until heated through. Season with salt and black pepper.

Serve over spaghettini. Sprinkle with Romano cheese.

Yield: 4 servings

PASTA, GRAINS & RICE

Gnocchi

6 large potatoes, peeled, cooked, mashed
1 teaspoon salt
Freshly ground pepper to taste
2 eggs, beaten
Freshly grated Parmesan cheese
4 cups unbleached flour
6 quarts water
2 tablespoons salt

Combine potatoes, 1 teaspoon salt, pepper, eggs and cheese in large bowl and mix well. Add 3 cups of the flour gradually, mixing well after each addition until a soft dough forms; use remaining flour to dust dough as needed while mixing.

Divide dough into 6 equal portions. Roll each into a thick rope. Cut into $1/2$-inch pieces; indent each piece lightly with fork to form ribs.

Bring water and 2 tablespoons salt to a boil in large saucepan. Drop in dough pieces. Cook for 2 to 3 minutes or until pieces float to top; drain well.

Top with melted butter or a savory sauce.

Yield: 4 servings

Spaetzle

2 cups (or more) flour
$1/2$ teaspoon salt
$1/8$ teaspoon nutmeg
2 eggs, beaten
$3/4$ to 1 cup milk
2 tablespoons butter

Sift flour, salt and nutmeg into large bowl. Add mixture of eggs and milk and mix until soft dough forms. Roll on lightly floured cutting board. Cut into $3/4$x2-inch slices.

Drop dough pieces into boiling water in 2- to 3-quart saucepan. Cook until dough floats to top. Remove to colander or bowl with sieve, strainer or large slotted spoon.

Sauté dough pieces in butter in skillet until heated through and lightly browned.

Serve with meat gravy or as a side dish with meat or vegetables.

Yield: 4 servings

PASTA, GRAINS & RICE

Baked Barley and Pine Nuts

1 cup barley, rinsed, drained
$^1/_3$ cup pine nuts
1 cup chopped green onions
4 to 6 tablespoons butter
$^1/_2$ bunch parsley, chopped
$^1/_4$ teaspoon salt
$^1/_4$ teaspoon pepper
$3^1/_3$ cups chicken broth

Sauté barley, pine nuts and green onions in butter in ovenproof skillet.

Add parsley, salt, pepper and chicken broth.

Bake at 350 degrees for $1^1/_2$ hours or until all the liquid is absorbed.

Yield: 8 servings

Mixed Grain Side Dish

1 medium onion, chopped
3 cups chicken stock or non-tomato-based vegetable stock
$^1/_2$ cup brown rice
$^1/_2$ cup jasmine or basmati rice
$^1/_2$ cup hulled barley
1 tablespoon snipped fresh sage
$^1/_2$ cup slivered blanched almonds
$^1/_2$ cup golden raisins
1 cup nonfat yogurt

Sauté onion in nonstick skillet until wilted.

Bring chicken stock to a boil in large saucepan. Add rice, barley, sage and onion. Simmer for 25 minutes or until liquid is absorbed.

Stir in almonds, raisins and yogurt. Cook until heated through.

Serve immediately.

Yield: 2 to 4 servings

Cajun Red Beans and Rice

1 pound smoked sausage, cut into $^1/_4$-inch slices
2 (15-ounce) cans red beans
1 teaspoon garlic powder
$^1/_4$ teaspoon oregano, or to taste
1 tablespoon Worcestershire sauce
1 teaspoon pepper
1 (8-ounce) can tomato sauce
1 (15-ounce) can water
Hot cooked rice

Brown sausage in Dutch oven; drain well.
Add beans, garlic powder, oregano, Worcestershire sauce, pepper and tomato sauce. Stir in water. Simmer for 30 to 45 minutes or until sausage is cooked through, adding additional water if needed.
Serve over rice.

Yield: 6 to 8 servings

Southwestern Rice Casserole

1 cup chopped onion
$^1/_4$ cup butter
4 cups freshly cooked white rice
2 cups sour cream
1 cup cream-style cottage cheese
1 large bay leaf
$^1/_2$ teaspoon salt
$^1/_8$ teaspoon pepper
2 (4-ounce) cans green chiles
2 cups shredded sharp Cheddar cheese
Chopped parsley

Sauté onion in butter in large skillet for 5 minutes. Remove from heat.
Stir in rice, sour cream, cottage cheese, bay leaf, salt and pepper, tossing lightly to mix well.
Layer rice mixture, chiles and cheese one-half at a time in lightly greased 8x12-inch baking dish.
Bake at 375 degrees for 25 minutes or until bubbly and heated through. Remove bay leaf before serving. Sprinkle with parsley.

Yield: 8 servings

Brown and White Rice Casserole

6 slices bacon, chopped
4 green onions, chopped
8 ounces fresh mushrooms, sliced
2 tablespoons butter
$^{1}/_{4}$ cup slivered almonds
$^{3}/_{4}$ cup brown rice
$^{3}/_{4}$ cup white rice
3 tablespoons butter
$^{1}/_{4}$ teaspoon salt
$^{1}/_{4}$ teaspoon pepper
$^{1}/_{4}$ teaspoon thyme
$^{1}/_{4}$ teaspoon marjoram
$3^{1}/_{4}$ cups beef broth
1 tablespoon butter
Grated Parmesan cheese

Cook bacon in skillet until crisp; drain and discard bacon drippings.

Sauté green onions and mushrooms in 2 tablespoons butter in same skillet until wilted. Remove and set aside.

Sauté almonds, brown rice and white rice in 3 tablespoons butter in same skillet until golden brown, stirring frequently.

Combine rice mixture, bacon, salt, pepper, thyme and marjoram in 2-quart casserole. Add beef broth and mix well.

Bake, covered, at 350 degrees for 40 minutes.

Stir in mushroom mixture. Adjust seasonings. Dot with 1 tablespoon butter; sprinkle with cheese.

Bake, covered, for 10 minutes longer.

Yield: 8 servings

Chinese Fried Rice

1 cup rice
Chicken broth or beef broth
$^{1}/_{4}$ cup vegetable oil
$^{1}/_{2}$ cup chopped chicken or pork
$^{1}/_{2}$ cup chopped shrimp
2 (or more) green onions, chopped
$^{1}/_{4}$ teaspoon sugar
1 tablespoon soy sauce
2 eggs, beaten
$^{1}/_{2}$ teaspoon salt
$^{1}/_{2}$ cup fresh or frozen peas
1 cup chopped bacon strips

Cook rice using package directions, substituting chicken broth or beef broth for water. Let cool.

Rinse chicken and pat dry. Heat oil in saucepan, wok or skillet. Add chicken, shrimp and green onions. Sauté for several minutes or until chicken is cooked through.

Add rice. Stir-fry until heated through. Stir in sugar and soy sauce.

Mix eggs with salt in bowl. Pour over rice mixture so that eggs coat rice and do not settle into lumps. Stir-fry for 3 minutes.

Add peas and bacon. Stir-fry until bacon is cooked through.

May add beef, veal or crab meat. May add additional vegetables.

Yield: 6 servings

PASTA, GRAINS & RICE

Mushroom Risotto

2 tablespoons dried porcini
mushrooms
6 tablespoons butter
1 pound mixed fresh
mushrooms, chopped
$^3/_4$ cup chopped sweet onion
1 clove of garlic, minced
$^1/_4$ cup white wine

$1^1/_2$ cups arborio rice
$^1/_2$ cup fresh-frozen peas, chopped
fresh asparagus or
chopped fresh spinach (optional)
2 cans chicken broth
$^1/_4$ cup freshly grated
Parmesan cheese

Soak dried mushrooms in water to cover for 20 minutes or until softened.

Melt butter in large heavy saucepan over medium heat. Add fresh mushrooms, onion and garlic. Cook until onion is translucent, stirring frequently.

Add wine and rice. Cook until rice is translucent and wine is evaporated.

Add undrained dried mushrooms and peas and mix well. Bring to a simmer. Add broth a small amount at a time, stirring constantly after each addition until broth is absorbed; process will take 20 to 40 minutes.

Add cheese and mix well.

Garnish with sprigs of fresh rosemary and additional Parmesan cheese.

Yield: 4 to 6 servings

Rice and Yuckni

12 ounces stewing beef, cut into cubes
1 small onion, cut into slivers
1 to 2 teaspoons butter
1 (16-ounce) can tomato sauce
$1^{1}/_{2}$ tomato sauce cans water
$^{1}/_{8}$ teaspoon salt, or to taste
$^{1}/_{8}$ teaspoon pepper, or to taste
1 teaspoon cinnamon
2 (16-ounce) cans green beans
Juice of $^{1}/_{2}$ lemon
3 to 4 cups cooked rice

Brown beef with onion in butter in saucepan.

Add tomato sauce, water, salt, pepper and cinnamon. Simmer, covered, for 45 to 60 minutes or until beef is tender.

Add green beans and mix well. Stir in lemon juice. Simmer for 10 minutes.

Serve over rice.

Yield: 6 servings

Syrian Rice

2 cups rice
Salt to taste
$^{1}/_{2}$ cup butter
Pine nuts to taste
8 ounces ground lamb
$^{3}/_{8}$ teaspoon cinnamon, or to taste
$^{1}/_{8}$ teaspoon cloves, or to taste
Boiling water

Soak rice in mixture of hot water and salt in bowl for 1 hour.

Melt butter in skillet. Add pine nuts. Cook over low heat until browned.

Add lamb. Cook until browned.

Drain and rinse rice. Add to lamb mixture. Add additional salt, cinnamon and cloves. Cook over low heat for 10 to 15 minutes, stirring often so rice does not stick.

Add enough boiling water to cover rice and mix well. Simmer, covered, over lowest heat for 20 minutes or until water is absorbed.

Add additional boiling water if rice is not done to taste; do not stir until ready to serve.

Yield: 4 to 6 servings

Wild Rice in Consommé

2 cups wild rice
$^{1}/_{2}$ cup butter
$^{1}/_{2}$ cup finely chopped onion
2 cups sliced mushrooms
2 cups consommé
2 cups water
$^{1}/_{2}$ cup chopped parsley
$^{3}/_{4}$ cup chopped red bell pepper

Rinse rice under running water and drain.

Melt butter in 3-quart saucepan. Add onion and mushrooms. Sauté briefly.

Add rice, consommé and water. Simmer, covered, over low heat for 1 hour or until liquid is absorbed.

Let stand, covered, for 15 minutes. Stir in parsley and red pepper.

Serve immediately.

Yield: 12 servings

Anytime Pesto

4 cups tightly packed parsley, or about
2 bunches, stems removed
4 large cloves of garlic
$^{1}/_{4}$ cup dried basil
$^{1}/_{4}$ cup walnuts
1 cup freshly grated Parmesan cheese
2 cups light olive oil
Salt and pepper to taste

Mince parsley in food processor. Add garlic, basil, walnuts and cheese. Process until well mixed.

Add olive oil in a stream with food processor running until sauce is thick and smooth, adding additional olive oil if needed and seasoning with salt and pepper.

Toss over fresh cooked pasta for a quick delicious meal.

Yield: 4 cups

Chinatown

Chicago's first Chinese settlement was a small community in the 1880s. The World's Columbian Exposition of 1893 saw an increase in the city's Chinese population, which necessitated a move from its original location. The present Chinatown, where only a small portion of Chicago's Chinese population lives, covers about twelve square blocks. It is a lively place to shop and eat authentic Chinese food and to watch the parade in celebration of Chinese New Year in early February.

A little Catholic church, originally built by Germans, was later used by Italians and now by Chinese. The street signs in Chinatown are lettered in both Chinese characters and English letters. The Chinatown community is a growing and prosperous one, with a good deal of cohesion, and new immigrants have helped to solidify the Asian presence in the city.

South of the famous Sears Tower is Chicago's own Chinatown

Chinese New Year Dinner

Szechuan Beef 152

Euro-Asian Eggplant 131

Spicy String Beans (Szechuan) 130

Chinese Fried Rice 120

Almond Crunch Cookies 212

VEGETABLES

Spicy String Beans (Szechuan)

Vegetables

Maverick Southern Grits à la Slightly North of the Border

4 cups water
$^1/_2$ teaspoon salt
1 tablespoon butter
1 to 1$^1/_2$ cups stone-ground grits
$^1/_4$ cup cream
1 tablespoon butter
1 ounce thinly sliced country ham
2 ounces smoked pork sausage,
cut into circles

1 teaspoon butter
6 shrimp, peeled, deveined
6 scallops, cleaned
$^1/_8$ teaspoon fresh garlic
$^1/_8$ teaspoon Cajun spice, or to taste
2 tablespoons chopped green onions
2 tablespoons chopped fresh tomato
1 tablespoon water
2 teaspoons butter

Bring 4 cups water, salt and 1 tablespoon butter to a boil in medium saucepan. Stir in 1 cup grits. Cook over low heat for 40 minutes or until grits are thick and creamy, stirring occasionally and adding more grits if needed to maintain consistency. Stir in cream and 1 tablespoon butter.

Sauté ham and sausage in 1 teaspoon butter in skillet until heated through.

Add shrimp and scallops. Sauté for 1 to 2 minutes. Add garlic and Cajun spice. Cook for 30 seconds.

Add green onions and tomato. Cook for 1 to 2 minutes or until heated through. Add 1 tablespoon water and 2 teaspoons butter. Cook for 1 to 2 minutes or until heated through. Pour over grits.

Yield: 2 to 4 servings

VEGETABLES

Bryant Gumbel's Sweet Corn Succotash

15 ears of fresh corn
10 slices bacon
6 cloves of garlic, chopped
6 green onions, chopped
2 tablespoons butter
1 green or red bell pepper, chopped
1 (16-ounce) can lima beans
1 small jar roasted peppers, chopped
1 large tomato, chopped
Salt and pepper to taste

Shuck corn and remove silk. Cut kernels from the cob into bowl using sharp knife.

Fry bacon in skillet until crisp; drain, reserving 1 tablespoon bacon drippings.

Sauté garlic and green onions in reserved bacon drippings in skillet until tender. Add butter and green pepper. Cook over medium heat until tender.

Add corn. Cook for 5 to 7 minutes or until heated through.

Add lima beans, roasted peppers and tomato and mix well. Crumble bacon into vegetable mixture. Season with salt and pepper.

Yield: 10 to 12 servings

Spicy String Beans (Szechuan)

1 ounce dried wood ear mushrooms
1 teaspoon each salt and sugar
1 tablespoon light soy sauce
1 tablespoon rice cooking wine
1 tablespoon sesame oil
4 cups water
1 tablespoon peanut or vegetable oil
1 1/2 pounds string beans, trimmed, cut into 2-inch pieces
2 tablespoons vegetable oil
3 cloves of garlic, finely chopped
4 to 5 fresh chiles, chopped
5 ounces bamboo shoots, cut into thin strips

Soak wood ear mushrooms in water to cover in bowl until softened. Cut into 1/4-inch strips.

Mix salt, sugar, soy sauce, wine and sesame oil in a small bowl. Bring 4 cups water and 1 tablespoon peanut oil to a boil in wok or saucepan. Add beans. Blanch for 1 minute. Drain and set aside.

Heat 2 tablespoons vegetable oil in wok until smoking. Add garlic, chiles and bamboo shoots and mix well. Add wood ears and beans. Stir-fry for 1 1/2 minutes. Add soy sauce mixture and mix well.

Serve immediately.

Variation (as seen in photograph on page 127): Use Chinese long beans (available in most Chinese markets). Trim ends but do not cut into pieces. Blanch as directed above. Fold in half and tie into knots. Continue as above. Garnish with butterfly-shaped pasta and red peppers.

Yield: 6 to 8 servings

VEGETABLES

Eggplant, Tomato and Goat Cheese Sandwiches

3 tablespoons olive oil
2 large cloves of garlic, minced
1 (12-inch-long) baguette piece
1 small eggplant
3 medium tomatoes
Salt and pepper to taste
3 ounces soft fresh Montrachet
or other goat cheese
12 fresh basil leaves

Combine olive oil and garlic in small bowl. Let stand for 5 minutes.

Cut bread into halves horizontally. Cut eggplant lengthwise into six $^1/_2$-inch slices. Cut tomatoes into 10 slices.

Brush cut sides of bread and both sides of eggplant and tomato slices with garlic mixture. Grill bread on grill rack over medium-high heat for 2 minutes or until toasted. Remove bread cut sides up to plates.

Season eggplant and tomato slices with salt and pepper. Grill eggplant on grill rack for 6 minutes per side or until cooked through. Remove to plates.

Grill tomatoes on grill rack for 1 minute per side or until heated through. Remove to plates.

Spread goat cheese over each bread half. Cover with overlapping eggplant slices. Top with tomato slices. Garnish with basil leaves.

Cut each sandwich diagonally into 4 sections.

Yield: 2 servings

Euro-Asian Eggplant

$^1/_4$ cup raisins
3 tablespoons olive oil
$^1/_2$ white onion, thinly sliced
2 medium eggplant, chopped
2 bay leaves
$^1/_4$ cup red wine vinegar
$^1/_2$ cup water
1 medium tomato, peeled, sliced
Salt and pepper to taste

Soak raisins in water to cover in small bowl for 30 minutes or longer; drain.

Heat olive oil in large skillet over medium heat. Add onion and eggplant. Sauté for 10 minutes. Add bay leaves, raisins and vinegar. Reduce heat to low.

Cook, covered, for 10 minutes or until vinegar evaporates. Add $^1/_2$ cup water, a small amount at a time. Cook for 30 minutes. Remove from heat and discard bay leaves. Stir in tomato. Season with salt and pepper.

Serve immediately.

Yield: 6 servings

Portobello Mushroom Burgers with Basil–Mustard Sauce

1¹/₂ cups mesquite wood
chips (optional)
1 cup cold water
1 cup mayonnaise
¹/₃ cup chopped fresh basil
2 tablespoons Dijon mustard
1 teaspoon fresh lemon juice
Salt and pepper to taste

¹/₃ cup olive oil
1 tablespoon minced garlic
6 (4- to 5-inch) portobello
mushrooms, stems removed
6 large whole-grain hamburger buns
6 large romaine leaves
6 large tomato slices

Soak wood chips in water for 1 hour.

Mix mayonnaise, basil, Dijon mustard and lemon juice in medium bowl. Season with salt and pepper.

Whisk olive oil with garlic in small bowl.

Drain wood chips and scatter over medium-hot coals. Brush mushroom caps with garlic mixture when wood chips begin to smoke. Season with salt and pepper. Grill on grill rack for 4 minutes per side or until tender and golden brown. Remove to platter and cover with foil to keep warm. Grill cut sides of buns on grill rack for 2 minutes or until golden brown.

Divide bottom halves of buns among 6 plates. Top each with 1 mushroom, 1 romaine leaf and 1 tomato slice. Spoon some of the basil-mustard sauce over tomatoes. Top with remaining buns.

Serve remaining basil-mustard sauce separately.

Yield: 6 servings

VEGETABLES

Sweet Chiles Rellenos

5 to 6 cloves of garlic, minced
2 teaspoons olive oil
5 (28-ounce) cans whole tomatoes, drained, peeled, seeded, chopped
$^1/_4$ teaspoon sugar
Salt to taste
2 tablespoons slivered fresh basil
Freshly ground pepper to taste
6 large fresh poblano chiles
$^1/_2$ white onion, minced
2 tablespoons canola or vegetable oil

8 ounces ground turkey
2 cloves of garlic, minced
2 small apples, chopped
1 pear, peeled, chopped
3 tablespoons raisins
1 plantain, heart removed, chopped
1 peach, peeled, chopped
2 tablespoons sugar
2 to 4 tablespoons flour
4 egg whites
3 egg yolks

Sauté 5 to 6 cloves of garlic in olive oil in 12-inch nonstick skillet over medium heat. Cook until garlic begins to color. Add tomatoes, $^1/_4$ teaspoon sugar and salt. Cook for 20 to 30 minutes or until tomatoes are cooked down and beginning to stick, stirring frequently. Remove from heat. Process 2 cups of tomato mixture in food processor for 30 seconds. Pour into saucepan. Stir in basil and pepper. Set aside.

Roast chiles over gas burner or under broiler until charred. Plunge into cold water in bowl immediately. Drain and remove skins. Slit lengthwise down one side and open out flat. Remove top stem and seeds, leaving veins in. Pat dry and set aside.

Sauté onion in canola oil in nonstick skillet over medium heat for 3 minutes or until onion is tender. Add turkey and 2 cloves of garlic. Cook until turkey is browned. Remove to large bowl.

Add unprocessed tomato mixture to skillet. Add fruits and 2 tablespoons sugar; stir gently. Cook until almost dry, stirring constantly. Stir in turkey mixture. Adjust seasonings.

Salt inside of chiles lightly. Place large spoonful of filling in each chile. Fold sides over so that they overlap; chiles should be packed as full as possible.

Roll chiles gently in flour to coat. Arrange chiles in single layer in large oiled gratin dish.

Beat egg whites in large mixer bowl until stiff but not dry. Beat egg yolks in medium mixer bowl. Fold egg yolks into egg whites. Spread over chiles. Bake at 400 degrees for 10 to 15 minutes or until browned. Heat processed tomato mixture. Ladle onto serving plate. Top with chiles. Serve immediately.

Yield: 6 servings

VEGETABLES

Trenette with Pesto, Potatoes and Green Beans

$^1/_4$ cup Italian parsley
$^3/_4$ cup packed fresh basil leaves
$^1/_2$ cup extra-virgin olive oil
6 tablespoons freshly grated
Pecorino Romano cheese
6 tablespoons freshly grated
Parmesan cheese
$^1/_4$ cup toasted pine nuts

$1^1/_2$ teaspoons minced garlic
Salt and pepper to taste
2 medium russet potatoes, peeled,
cut into $^1/_2$-inch cubes
6 ounces green beans, trimmed,
cut into 3-inch pieces
1 pound trenette or linguini

Combine parsley, basil, olive oil, cheeses, pine nuts and garlic in food processor container. Process until finely ground. Season with salt and pepper.

Cook potatoes in boiling salted water in large saucepan for 5 minutes or just until tender. Remove to large bowl using slotted spoon.

Add green beans to saucepan. Cook for 3 minutes or until tender-crisp. Remove to bowl with potatoes using slotted spoon.

Add pasta to saucepan. Cook until tender but still firm to taste. Drain, reserving $^1/_2$ cup cooking liquid. Add pasta to potatoes and green beans.

Whisk reserved cooking liquid into pesto. Add pesto to pasta mixture, tossing thoroughly to coat.

Transfer to large platter. Serve immediately, passing additional freshly grated Pecorino Romano cheese separately.

Pesto may be prepared up to 2 days ahead. Press plastic wrap onto surface and refrigerate until needed.

Yield: 4 servings

VEGETABLES

Green Bean Casserole

3 (20-ounce) cans green beans, drained
1 medium red onion, cut into rings
8 slices bacon
6 tablespoons sugar
6 tablespoons cider vinegar
$^1/_2$ cup slivered almonds

Place beans in $1^1/_2$-quart casserole. Top with red onion rings.

Fry bacon in skillet until crisp; drain, reserving drippings. Crumble bacon over onions.

Combine sugar, vinegar and reserved drippings in saucepan. Cook until heated through. Pour over beans.

Marinate, covered, in refrigerator for several hours to overnight, stirring occasionally.

Top with almonds. Bake at 350 degrees for 45 minutes.

Yield: 6 servings

Italian Stuffed Peppers

2 cups bread crumbs
$^1/_2$ cup vegetable oil
$^1/_4$ tablespoon grated Parmesan cheese
$^1/_3$ cup chopped pine nuts
Salt and pepper to taste
6 small green or red bell peppers, cut into halves lengthwise

Combine bread crumbs, oil, cheese, pine nuts, salt and pepper in bowl and mix well. Spoon into peppers. Place peppers in nonstick baking pan.

Bake at 350 degrees for 30 minutes.

May add $^1/_2$ cup niblet corn and $^1/_2$ cup mozzarella cheese cubes to stuffing. Bake, covered with foil, for 15 minutes. Uncover and bake for 15 minutes longer.

Yield: 6 servings

VEGETABLES

New Potatoes with Herbs

3 to 4 pounds red potatoes, cut into
bite-size pieces
1 medium Vidalia or other sweet onion,
cut into large chunks
$^1/_2$ cup olive oil
1 to 2 large cloves of garlic, minced
2 tablespoons fresh rosemary
1 teaspoon thyme
1 teaspoon sage
$^1/_4$ teaspoon salt
Freshly ground black pepper to taste
1 to 2 teaspoons red pepper

Arrange potatoes and onion in 9x13-inch
baking dish.

Mix olive oil, garlic, rosemary, thyme, sage, salt,
black pepper and red pepper in bowl. Pour over
potatoes and onion, tossing to mix.

Bake at 450 degrees for 35 to 40 minutes or until
potatoes are tender, turning every 15 minutes.

Yield: 6 to 8 servings

Spicy Bacon, Onion and Cheese Potatoes

8 slices bacon, coarsely chopped
2 pounds russet potatoes, peeled,
cut into $^1/_2$-inch pieces
1 large onion, chopped
Salt and pepper to taste
1 cup packed shredded hot pepper Monterey
Jack cheese
2 tablespoons butter

Cook bacon in large heavy skillet over medium
heat until crisp and browned. Remove bacon to
paper towels using slotted spoon; drain well.

Combine bacon, potatoes and onion in buttered
9x13-inch glass baking dish and mix well. Season
with salt and pepper. Sprinkle with cheese. Dot
with butter.

Bake, covered with foil, at 350 degrees for 1 hour
or until potatoes and onion are very tender.

Broil, uncovered, for 2 minutes or until top is
browned and crisp.

Yield: 8 servings

VEGETABLES

*Chinatown's colorful
annual New Year's
parade*

137

New American Fries

2 large russet potatoes, peeled or unpeeled
1 tablespoon olive oil

Cut potatoes into thin slices with food processor or mandoline. Place potatoes on large oiled baking sheet. Brush with olive oil.

Place baking sheet 6 inches from heat source. Broil for 10 to 12 minutes or until golden brown, turning after 7 minutes.

Remove to platter using spatula. Serve immediately with catsup or other condiments of your choice.

Yield: 2 to 3 servings

Oven-Roasted Potato Fries

6 large red, white or russet potatoes
Seasoned salt to taste
Thyme, rosemary and paprika to taste
Ground rock salt and freshly ground pepper to taste
$^1/_4$ cup olive oil
$^1/_2$ cup minced chives (optional)

Cut potatoes into halves; cut each half lengthwise into 5 to 6 finger-like wedges. Arrange in large heavy baking dish. Season to taste.

Pour olive oil over potatoes. Bake, covered with foil, at 425 degrees for 45 minutes. Stir well. Bake, uncovered, for 45 minutes, turning once. Sprinkle with chives.

Yield: 6 servings

VEGETABLES

Savory Potato Fries

1 envelope onion-mushroom soup mix
2 teaspoons thyme
1 teaspoon marjoram
$^1/_4$ teaspoon pepper
2 pounds potatoes, cut into quarters

Combine the soup mix, thyme, marjoram and pepper in a paper bag. Add potatoes, shaking to coat well.

Arrange potatoes on baking sheet sprayed with nonstick cooking spray. Bake at 400 degrees for 30 to 50 minutes or until tender and browned.

Yield: 6 to 8 servings

Easy Oven-Baked Hash Browns

6 large red potatoes
1 small onion, thinly sliced
2 large cloves of garlic, minced
$^1/_4$ cup olive oil
Ground rock salt and freshly ground pepper to taste
Paprika to taste
1 tablespoon minced parsley
1 tablespoon margarine, cut into small pieces (optional)

Steam potatoes in steamer or saucepan. Peel and cut into thin slices.

Arrange potatoes in lightly oiled baking dish. Add onion, garlic, olive oil, salt and pepper and toss well. Dust with paprika and parsley. Dot with margarine.

Bake at 450 degrees for 15 minutes. Turn potatoes with spatula. Decrease oven temperature to 350 degrees. Bake for 30 to 60 minutes or until potatoes are tender.

Potatoes can remain in 300-degree oven for up to 2 hours.

Yield: 3 to 4 servings

VEGETABLES

Spiced Sweet Potatoes

6 medium sweet potatoes
$^1/_2$ teaspoon ground cinnamon
$^1/_2$ teaspoon ground ginger
$^1/_2$ teaspoon ground nutmeg
$^1/_2$ teaspoon ground cloves
$^1/_2$ teaspoon salt
$^1/_4$ cup unsalted butter, cut into pieces
3 tablespoons honey

Boil sweet potatoes in water to cover in saucepan until tender. Peel and cut into $^1/_2$-inch slices.

Mix cinnamon, ginger, nutmeg, cloves and salt in bowl.

Layer sweet potatoes in 2x10-inch round baking dish, sprinkling each layer with some of the spice mixture, dotting with butter and drizzling with honey.

Bake at 375 degrees for 20 minutes or until heated through.

Yield: 6 to 8 servings

Broiled Yam Chips

2 medium yams, cut into $^1/_8$-inch slices
2 tablespoons sunflower oil
Salt-free seasoning (optional)

Arrange yam slices close together but not overlapping on 2 lightly oiled baking sheets. Brush with sunflower oil. Sprinkle with seasoning.

Broil close to heat source for 10 minutes or until lightly browned.

Yield: 4 servings

VEGETABLES

Sweet Potato Streusel Squares

3 pounds sweet potatoes, peeled,
cut into 1-inch pieces
Salt to taste
$^1/_4$ cup butter, at room temperature
$^1/_4$ cup sugar
1 cup half-and-half
2 eggs
$^1/_3$ cup chopped crystallized ginger
1 teaspoon vanilla extract
1 cup packed light brown sugar
$^1/_2$ cup flour
$^1/_2$ cup butter, at room temperature
1 cup chopped pecans
1 cup sweetened flaked coconut

Cook sweet potatoes in boiling salted water in large saucepan for 8 minutes or until tender; drain and return to saucepan. Cook over medium-high heat until excess liquid evaporates, stirring constantly. Remove from heat.

Add $^1/_4$ cup butter and sugar. Mash sweet potatoes until almost smooth. Add half-and-half, eggs, ginger and vanilla and mix well. Season with salt. Spread in buttered 9x13-inch glass baking dish.

Rub brown sugar, flour and $^1/_2$ cup butter in a bowl until moist crumbs form. Stir in pecans and coconut. Sprinkle over sweet potato mixture.

Bake at 350 degrees for 40 minutes or until filling is set and topping is browned. Let stand for 10 minutes. Cut into squares.

Yield: 12 servings

Sautéed Squash

2 tablespoons margarine
1 tablespoon olive oil
2 yellow squash, coarsely grated
2 zucchini, coarsely grated
Salt and pepper to taste
1 tablespoon snipped parsley
2 cloves of garlic, minced

Heat margarine and olive oil in wok or skillet. Add squash and zucchini. Cook for 5 minutes or until tender.

Add salt, pepper, parsley and garlic. Cook for 2 minutes.

Serve immediately.

Yield: 6 servings

Gratin of Cherry Tomatoes

1¹/₂ pints cherry tomatoes
Salt and freshly ground pepper to taste
2 teaspoons herbes de Provence
2 large cloves of garlic, minced
2 large slices white or French bread
¹/₂ cup coarsely chopped parsley
¹/₂ cup freshly grated Parmesan cheese
¹/₄ cup fruit-flavored olive oil

Cut a thin sliver from stem end of each tomato so that it will lie flat. Arrange compactly in single layer in baking dish. Season with salt, pepper and herbes de Provence.

Combine garlic, bread, parsley and cheese in food processor container. Process until coarse crumbs form. Add olive oil in a stream, processing constantly until mixture is evenly moistened. Sprinkle over tomatoes.

Bake at 400 degrees for 40 to 45 minutes or until crumbs are crusty brown and juices from tomatoes are bubbly. Cool for several minutes before serving.

Yield: 6 servings

Fresh and Dried Tomato Topping

6 tablespoons extra-virgin olive oil
6 oil-packed sun-dried tomatoes, chopped
2 large cloves of garlic, minced
3 to 4 fresh basil leaves
³/₄ teaspoon salt
Freshly ground pepper to taste
2 medium tomatoes, seeded, chopped

Heat olive oil in skillet. Add sun-dried tomatoes, garlic, basil, salt and pepper. Cook gently for 4 minutes or until garlic is tender.

Add fresh tomatoes. Cook for 1 minute or until heated through. Adjust seasonings.

Use on any basic Italian flatbread. Sprinkle with freshly grated Parmesan cheese and broil.

Yield: 1¹/₄ cups

Sun-Dried Tomato Chutney

Do not use oil-packed tomatoes in this recipe.

$^1/_3$ cup sun-dried tomatoes
1 small tart apple, peeled, finely chopped
$^1/_3$ cup finely chopped onion
$^1/_3$ cup finely chopped cooked ham
$^1/_4$ cup finely chopped red bell pepper
3 tablespoons brown sugar
3 tablespoons apple cider vinegar
2 tablespoons finely chopped raisins
$^1/_2$ teaspoon crushed dried basil
1 clove of garlic, minced
$^1/_2$ teaspoon crushed red pepper

Combine tomatoes and boiling water to cover in small bowl. Let stand for 10 minutes; drain, reserving 2 tablespoons soaking liquid. Snip or finely chop tomatoes.

Combine tomatoes, apple, onion, ham, red bell pepper, brown sugar, vinegar, raisins, reserved liquid, basil, garlic and crushed red pepper in small saucepan. Bring to a boil; reduce heat. Simmer for 15 minutes, stirring occasionally.

Let stand, covered, at room temperature for 30 minutes. Chill, covered, until serving time.

Yield: $2^1/_2$ cups

Stir-Fry Vegetables (Hunan)

$^1/_8$ ounce dried cloud ear mushrooms
4 ounces pea pods
2 tablespoons chili paste with garlic
1 teaspoon salt
1 teaspoon sugar
1 tablespoon rice vinegar
1 tablespoon rice cooking wine
1 tablespoon cornstarch
2 tablespoons peanut or vegetable oil
3 cloves of garlic, finely chopped
5 ounces bamboo shoots, sliced
5 ounces water chestnuts, sliced
4 ounces red bell peppers,
cut into $^5/_8$-inch pieces
4 ounces green bell peppers,
cut into $^5/_8$-inch pieces
$^1/_2$ cup chicken broth
2 tablespoons shrimp powder

Soak cloud ear mushrooms in water to cover for 20 minutes; drain and set aside.

Remove the fiber from both ends of pea pods.

Mix chili paste, salt, sugar, vinegar, wine and cornstarch in bowl; set aside.

Heat oil in wok until smoking. Add garlic, bamboo shoots, water chestnuts, cloud ear mushrooms, bell peppers and pea pods and mix well. Add the chicken broth. Cook, covered, for 3 minutes. Add the wine mixture and mix well.

Place on serving platter. Sprinkle with shrimp powder.

Yield: 6 to 8 servings

3639

NEIGHBO

Wrigleyville

Beyond the ivy-covered walls of Wrigley Field, home of the Chicago Cubs, lie the streets, sidewalks and rooftops of Wrigleyville. During the summer, crowds flock to the corner of Clark and Addison to watch baseball in a largely unchanged setting.

Wrigleyville and baseball have grown together hand in glove. Before the turn of the century, Lakeview, of which Wrigleyville is a part, was considered to be so far from the city that it was a summer colony. By 1914, when the ballpark opened, the elevated train and trolley lines had brought business and workers to the area. German and Swedish tradesmen moved north to this area and built brick and greystone two and three flats.

Today, Wrigleyville maintains a lively spirit, resulting from an influx of younger people and diverse cultures. A variety of ethnic restaurants tempt local diners, but a picnic, barbecue or hot dog is best suited for a day at the ball park.

A rooftop party overlooking Wrigley Field on game day

Rooftop Barbecue

Black Bean Salsa 17

Chips

Honey Bourbon Grilled Pork Tenderloin 163

New American Fries 138

Bryant Gumbel's Sweet Corn Succotash 130

Grilled Mixed Vegetables

Peach Shortcake 227

Honey Bourbon Grilled Pork Tenderloin

Meats

Sauerbraten

2$^1/_2$ cups water
$^3/_4$ cup red wine vinegar
2 medium onions, sliced
1 lemon, sliced
12 cloves of garlic, minced
6 black peppercorns, crushed
4 bay leaves, crushed
1 tablespoon sugar

$^1/_4$ teaspoon ground ginger
1 (1-pound) boneless beef rump
roast or other pot roast
2 tablespoons vegetable oil
$^1/_2$ cup chopped onion
$^1/_2$ cup chopped carrot
1$^1/_2$ cups broken gingersnaps
$^2/_3$ cup (about) water

Combine 2$^1/_2$ cups water, vinegar, sliced onions, lemon, garlic, peppercorns, bay leaves, sugar, ginger and beef in large plastic container with airtight lid. Marinate in refrigerator for 2 to 3 days, shaking or turning daily.

Remove beef from marinade and pat dry. Strain and reserve remaining marinade.

Heat oil in Dutch oven. Add beef. Cook until browned; drain well. Add reserved marinade, chopped onion and carrot. Simmer, covered, for 2 hours or until beef is tender. Remove beef to platter and keep warm.

Pour off and discard all but 2 cups cooking liquid. Add gingersnaps and $^2/_3$ cup water to vegetables and cooking liquid in Dutch oven. Cook until mixture is thickened and bubbly and gingersnaps have dissolved, stirring constantly.

Slice beef crossgrain. Return to Dutch oven to warm.

Serve over hot cooked noodles or mashed potatoes.

Yield: 6 to 8 servings

MEATS

Italian Beef

1 (4-pound) rump roast
1 large onion, sliced
1 cup cider vinegar
2 tablespoons oregano
2 teaspoons garlic salt
2 tablespoons Worcestershire sauce
4 cups water
1 (16-ounce) jar peperoncinis in vinegar

Place roast in roasting pan. Top with onion slices.

Combine vinegar, oregano, garlic salt, Worcestershire sauce and water in large bowl and mix well. Pour over roast. Bake, covered, at 275 degrees for 3 hours or to desired degree of doneness. Let cool. Cut into very thin slices. Return to roasting pan.

Add undrained peppers to pan drippings and mix well. Bake, covered, for 2 hours longer.

Serve beef over toasted rolls with sauce for dipping.

Yield: 10 to 15 servings

Filet Mignon with Madeira Sauce

4 (8-ounce) filets mignons
Salt and pepper to taste
2 tablespoons olive oil
2 tablespoons finely chopped shallots
$^1/_2$ cup madeira
$^3/_4$ cup beef broth
2 teaspoons butter
1 teaspoon flour
1 teaspoon butter
2 teaspoons chopped parsley

Sprinkle steaks with salt and pepper. Heat olive oil in large skillet until very hot. Add filets. Cook over high heat for 10 minutes or until done to taste, turning once. Remove to warm platter and keep warm.

Drain skillet. Add shallots and wine to skillet. Cook over high heat for 30 seconds. Add beef broth. Bring to full rolling boil. Season with additional salt and pepper. Cook until reduced by half.

Blend 2 teaspoons butter and flour in small bowl. Stir into simmering sauce. Cook briefly. Swirl in 1 teaspoon butter.

Strain sauce over filets. Sprinkle with parsley. Serve immediately.

Yield: 4 servings

MEATS

London Broil à la Junior League of Chicago

2 tablespoons sesame seeds
1 tablespoon butter
$^1/_2$ cup strong coffee
$^1/_2$ cup soy sauce
1 tablespoon Worcestershire sauce
1 tablespoon cider vinegar
1 medium onion, chopped
1 (3-inch) sirloin or top round steak

Brown sesame seeds in butter in skillet. Combine with coffee, soy sauce, Worcestershire sauce, vinegar and onion in bowl and mix well.

Place steak in sealable plastic bag. Pour in marinade. Marinate in refrigerator for 8 to 10 hours, turning occasionally. Remove steak and reserve remaining marinade.

Grill steak over medium-hot coals to desired degree of doneness, basting occasionally with reserved marinade.

Yield: 6 to 8 servings

Steak au Poivre

3 tablespoons black peppercorns, cracked
4 boneless steaks
$1^1/_2$ tablespoons olive oil
$1^1/_2$ tablespoons unsalted butter
$^1/_4$ cup minced shallots
$^1/_2$ cup Cognac
1 cup beef broth
$^2/_3$ cup whipping cream
Sprigs of watercress

Crush peppercorns and press into both sides of steaks. Let stand at room temperature for 1 hour.

Heat olive oil and butter in large skillet until foam subsides. Add steaks. Sauté for 2 to $2^1/_2$ minutes per side or to desired degree of doneness. Set steaks aside and keep warm.

Drain most of the pan drippings from skillet. Add shallots. Cook until softened.

Add Cognac. Boil until mixture is reduced to glaze consistency. Add beef broth. Boil until reduced by half. Add whipping cream. Boil until slightly thickened, stirring occasionally.

Pour sauce over steaks. Top with watercress.

Yield: 4 servings

MEATS

Baked Chop Suey

3 pounds meat of your choice,
cut into bite-size pieces
3 cups coarsely chopped onions
4 cups chopped celery
1 (8-ounce) can sliced mushrooms
1 can sliced bamboo shoots, drained
1 can sliced water chestnuts, drained
1 can bean sprouts, rinsed, drained
1 teaspoon salt
5 tablespoons soy sauce
2$^1/_2$ tablespoons bead molasses
1 tablespoon (heaping) cornstarch

Layer the meat, onions, celery, undrained mushrooms, bamboo shoots, water chestnuts and bean sprouts in large casserole. Sprinkle with salt. Drizzle with soy sauce; do not stir.

Bake, tightly covered, at 275 degrees for 3 hours. Drizzle with molasses and stir well. Bake, tightly covered, for 1 hour longer.

Mix cornstarch with a small amount of cold water. Add to beef mixture gradually, mixing well after each addition until liquid is of desired consistency.

Yield: 6 to 8 servings

Szechuan Beef

6 tablespoons low-sodium soy sauce
3 tablespoons dry sherry
2 tablespoons cornstarch
2 tablespoons dried or fresh ginger
5 to 12 dried red peppers
Vegetable oil
1 pound steak, cut into $^1/_2$-inch cubes
4 to 6 carrots, julienned
1 can bamboo shoots

Mix soy sauce, sherry, cornstarch and ginger in bowl and set aside.

Brown peppers in a small amount of oil in skillet or wok. Add steak. Cook until browned. Set aside.

Stir-fry carrots in a small amount of oil in skillet or wok for 2 to 4 minutes or until tender. Add bamboo shoots. Stir-fry for 1 minute.

Add sauce and steak mixture. Cook until sauce is thickened, stirring constantly.

Serve with rice.

Yield: 4 servings

Savory Casserole

1^{1}/$_{2}$ large onions, chopped
1 clove of garlic, minced
8 ounces mushrooms, sliced
^{1}/$_{2}$ cup butter
1 pound cubed beef or veal
1 pound cubed pork
^{1}/$_{2}$ cup wild rice
^{1}/$_{2}$ cup white rice
1 can consommé

^{1}/$_{4}$ cup soy sauce
2 cups chopped celery
1 can water chestnuts
2 teaspoons seasoned salt
1 can consommé
^{1}/$_{2}$ cup slivered almonds or whole cashews
1 teaspoon butter

Sauté onions, garlic and mushrooms in ^{1}/$_{2}$ cup butter in skillet. Remove from heat. Add beef and pork. Cook until lightly browned.

Combine beef mixture, wild rice, white rice, 1 can consommé, soy sauce, celery, water chestnuts and seasoned salt in large casserole and mix well.

Bake at 350 degrees for 2 hours. Heat remaining consommé in saucepan. Stir into baked mixture. Bake for 25 minutes longer.

Brown the almonds in 1 teaspoon butter in skillet. Sprinkle over casserole. Bake for 5 minutes longer.

Serve with salad.

Yield: 6 servings

MEATS

Beef Fajitas

1 1/2 pounds beef top round steak
or pepper steak
2 cups tomato juice
1/3 cup lime juice
2 tablespoons bottled hot
pepper sauce
2 cloves of garlic, finely
chopped or crushed

2 tomatoes, coarsely chopped
1 large red onion, coarsely chopped
1 large red bell pepper,
coarsely chopped
1 bunch fresh cilantro, chopped
12 (10-inch) flour tortillas
1/2 cup sour cream
1/2 cup shredded Cheddar cheese

Trim excess fat from steak. Cut into halves lengthwise; cut crossgrain into strips. Place in large glass baking dish.

Mix tomato juice, lime juice, hot pepper sauce and garlic in bowl. Pour over steak. Marinate in refrigerator for 4 to 24 hours, stirring occasionally.

Arrange tomatoes, onion, red pepper and cilantro on serving platter. Refrigerate, covered with plastic wrap, until needed.

Drain marinade into saucepan. Cook over high heat for 10 minutes or until slightly thickened, stirring occasionally.

Wrap tortillas in foil. Warm in 350-degree oven for 10 minutes.

Broil a few steak strips at a time 2 inches from heat source for 4 minutes, turning once. Set aside and keep warm.

Serve steak strips on platter with warm tortillas, vegetables, sauce, sour cream and cheese. Allow each person to prepare fajitas as desired.

Yield: 6 servings

MEATS

Shepherd's Pie

1 pound potatoes, peeled, cut into cubes
1 small onion, chopped
2 tablespoons butter
1 pound cooked minced beef
2 tomatoes, chopped
$^1/_2$ cup beef stock
Salt and pepper to taste
1 egg, beaten

Cook potatoes in boiling water to cover until tender; drain and mash.

Sauté onion in butter in a skillet. Stir in beef. Add tomatoes, beef stock, salt and pepper and mix well. Pour into large casserole. Cover with mashed potatoes. Brush with a small amount of egg.

Bake at 350 degrees for 20 minutes.

May substitute cooked sliced potatoes or almost any leftover vegetables for mashed potatoes.

Yield: 4 to 6 servings

Sesame Sauce for Beef

1 cup soy sauce
$^1/_2$ cup dry sherry
$^1/_2$ cup sugar
$^1/_2$ cup catsup
1 teaspoon garlic powder
1 teaspoon onion powder
1 teaspoon ground ginger
1 tablespoon sesame oil
Star anise to taste
Toasted sesame seeds to taste
Sliced green onions to taste
1 tablespoon cornstarch
2 tablespoons cold water

Combine soy sauce, sherry, sugar, catsup, garlic powder, onion powder, ginger, sesame oil, star anise, sesame seeds and green onions in saucepan. Bring to a boil; reduce heat. Simmer for 10 minutes, stirring occasionally.

Stir in mixture of cornstarch and cold water to thicken slightly.

Use as marinade for beef or as sauce on the side.

Yield: $2^1/_2$ cups

MEATS

Amazing Meat Loaf

$^{1}/_{2}$ ounce dried porcini mushrooms
$^{1}/_{4}$ cup hot water
$^{1}/_{2}$ cup thinly sliced carrot
$^{1}/_{2}$ cup sliced fresh mushrooms
$^{1}/_{2}$ cup chopped yellow onion
1 teaspoon minced garlic
1 tablespoon olive oil
1 egg
$^{1}/_{2}$ cup catsup
$^{1}/_{4}$ cup Worcestershire sauce

1 teaspoon hot pepper sauce
2 pounds ground
sirloin or turkey
$^{1}/_{2}$ cup bread crumbs
1 teaspoon thyme
1 teaspoon sage
$^{1}/_{2}$ teaspoon marjoram
1 teaspoon pepper
2 to 3 tablespoons catsup

Soak porcini mushrooms in hot water for 20 minutes or until softened; drain, reserving soaking liquid.

Sauté carrot, fresh mushrooms, onion and garlic in olive oil in skillet until onion is translucent and carrot is tender; do not brown. Add porcini mushrooms. Sauté lightly.

Mix egg, $^{1}/_{2}$ cup catsup, Worcestershire sauce, hot pepper sauce and sirloin in large bowl. Mix bread crumbs, thyme, sage, marjoram and pepper in small bowl. Add to sirloin mixture and mix well. Stir in sautéed vegetable mixture and 1 tablespoon reserved liquid.

Shape into loaf and place in loaf pan. Mix 1 tablespoon reserved liquid with 2 to 3 tablespoons catsup in bowl. Pour over meat loaf.

Bake at 375 degrees for 1 hour.

Serve with a root vegetable purée.

Yield: 4 servings

MEATS

Wrigley Field, home of the Chicago Cubs

Dolmathes (Stuffed Grape Leaves)

1/2 cup rice
1 large onion, chopped
2 tablespoons melted butter
1 pound ground steak
1/2 cup chopped parsley
1/2 cup chopped mint
2 teaspoons salt

Pepper to taste
50 fresh or canned grape
leaves, rinsed
1 tablespoon butter
Salt to taste
3 eggs
Juice of 1 lemon

Soak rice in cold water to cover.

Fry onion in 2 tablespoons butter in skillet until golden brown. Drain rice. Combine onion, rice, steak, parsley, mint, salt and pepper in large bowl and mix well.

Place 1 teaspoon filling in center of 1 large or 2 small grape leaves, making sure shiny side of leaf faces down. Fold over top and sides as for an envelope. Roll in shape of miniature football. Repeat process until all filling is used.

Place a few coarse grape leaves in large stockpot. Add rolled leaves in layers. Add enough water to cover rolls, 1 tablespoon butter and additional salt. Place heavy heatproof plate over rolls to hold them down. Simmer for 30 minutes or until filling is heated through and steak is cooked to desired degree of doneness. Drain, reserving 5 to 6 tablespoons cooking liquid in small bowl. Keep rolls warm over low heat.

Beat eggs lightly in bowl. Add lemon juice and beat well. Add to reserved liquid 1 tablespoon at a time, beating well after each addition. Pour over grape leaf rolls. Allow sauce to heat but not boil.

Remove from heat. Serve hot.

Yield: 4 to 8 servings

MEATS

Veal Osso Buco

4 large veal shanks
$^1/_4$ cup flour
2 tablespoons olive oil
1 cup carrot, sliced $^1/_4$ inch thick
1 cup celery, sliced $^1/_4$ inch thick
1 large onion, sliced $^1/_4$ inch thick
2 (14-ounce) cans stewed
tomatoes, crushed

3 tablespoons tomato sauce
6 bay leaves
$^1/_2$ teaspoon lemon pepper
1 teaspoon parsley flakes
1 teaspoon grated lemon peel
2 large cloves of garlic, crushed
1 cup (or more) dry white wine

Cut veal 2$^1/_2$ inches thick and 2$^1/_2$ inches in diameter. Pat veal dry and dust lightly with flour.

Heat olive oil in 5-quart Dutch oven. Add veal. Sauté until lightly browned.

Mix carrots, celery, onion and undrained tomatoes in bowl. Add to Dutch oven. Add tomato sauce, pushing tomato sauce lightly into vegetable mixture with spoon. Add bay leaves in random spacing. Sprinkle with lemon pepper, parsley flakes, lemon peel and garlic. Add enough wine to cover veal and vegetables.

Simmer, covered, for 3 hours or until sauce is slightly reduced and veal is tender. Remove bay leaves.

Place 1 veal shank in center of each plate. Surround with vegetables. Spoon some sauce and a few vegetables over each veal shank.

Yield: 4 servings

MEATS

Lemon Veal

2 pounds veal scallops
$^1/_2$ cup flour
2 teaspoons salt
$^1/_2$ teaspoon freshly ground black pepper
$^1/_8$ teaspoon cayenne, or to taste
$^1/_4$ cup butter
$^1/_4$ cup vegetable oil
$^1/_4$ cup butter
1 tablespoon fresh tarragon, or $^1/_4$ teaspoon
dried (optional)
5 tablespoons freshly squeezed lemon juice
5 tablespoons chopped fresh parsley
1 lemon, thinly sliced

Pound veal between sheets of waxed paper to flatten. Mix flour, salt, black pepper and cayenne in sealable plastic bag. Add veal, shaking to coat evenly.

Brown veal in $^1/_4$ cup butter and oil in skillet; do not overcook. Remove veal; drain skillet. Melt remaining $^1/_4$ cup butter in skillet. Add tarragon, lemon juice and parsley. Bring to a simmer. Add veal, turning to coat with sauce.

Top with lemon slices and additional parsley. Serve immediately.

Yield: 6 servings

Psito Arni Sto Harti (Baked Lamb in Foil)

2 tablespoons olive oil
1 onion, chopped
1 tomato, chopped
$^1/_8$ teaspoon salt, or to taste
$^1/_8$ teaspoon pepper, or to taste
$^1/_8$ teaspoon dillseeds, or to taste
3 pounds lamb, cut into serving-size pieces
1 pound feta cheese, cut into pieces

Heat olive oil in skillet. Add onion. Sauté briefly. Add tomato, salt, pepper and dillseeds. Sauté until onion is golden brown.

Place each piece of lamb on a foil square. Spoon sauce over lamb. Top with 2 pieces of cheese. Wrap securely and place in large baking dish.

Bake at 375 degrees for 2 hours or until tender.

Yield: 6 to 8 servings

Lamb Burgers with Yogurt Sauce

8 ounces ground lamb
$^1/_4$ teaspoon cumin
$^1/_4$ teaspoon paprika
$^1/_4$ cup goat cheese
1 tablespoon butter
$^1/_2$ cup plain yogurt
2 tablespoons minced green onions
3 drops of hot pepper sauce
Salt and freshly ground white pepper to taste

Mix lamb, cumin and paprika in bowl. Shape into 2 large patties. Place 2 tablespoons cheese in center of each patty. Fold over into semicircles, then into ovals that completely cover the cheese.

Melt butter in skillet over medium-high heat. Add burgers. Cook for 5 minutes per side or until cooked through.

Blend yogurt, green onions, hot pepper sauce, salt and white pepper in bowl.

Place each burger in a pita; spoon yogurt sauce over burgers.

Yield: 2 servings

Pork Chops

4 pork chops
1 tablespoon vegetable oil
2 cloves of garlic, minced
4 teaspoons vegetable oil
$^1/_2$ cup sherry or broth
$^1/_2$ cup soy sauce
$^1/_4$ cup packed brown sugar
$^1/_2$ teaspoon crushed red pepper
4 teaspoons cornstarch
$^1/_4$ cup water

Trim excess fat from pork chops. Heat 1 tablespoon oil in skillet. Add pork chops. Cook until browned. Remove pork chops and add garlic to skillet. Sauté for 1 minute.

Mix 4 teaspoons oil, sherry, soy sauce, brown sugar and red pepper in bowl. Return pork chops to skillet. Pour sauce over chops. Simmer, tightly covered, over low heat for 30 to 35 minutes or until tender and cooked through, turning once and adding a small amount of water if needed to keep sauce from cooking down too much. Remove pork chops from skillet.

Dissolve cornstarch in water and stir into sauce. Cook until thickened. Arrange pork chops over bed of cooked noodles. Pour sauce over pork chops.

Yield: 4 servings

MEATS

Marinade for Lamb, Pork Roast or Duck

1 clove of garlic, crushed
1 tablespoon chopped fresh cilantro
2 teaspoons salt
$1/4$ teaspoon cayenne
$1/4$ cup white wine vinegar
$1/2$ cup dry red wine
$1/4$ cup extra-virgin olive oil

Combine garlic, cilantro, salt and cayenne in large bowl. Stir in vinegar and wine. Whisk in olive oil gradually.

Meat should be marinated in refrigerator for 12 hours. Drain marinade and chill for 2 to 3 hours before grilling.

Yield: 1 cup

Stuffed Pork Tenderloin

1 pork loin, split into halves
4 to 5 slices white bread, crusts trimmed,
cut into cubes
$1/2$ teaspoon poultry seasoning
$1/2$ teaspoon thyme
$1/2$ teaspoon marjoram
$1/2$ teaspoon sage
1 teaspoon celery seeds
$1/8$ teaspoon pepper
$3/4$ teaspoon salt
$1/2$ cup butter
$1/4$ cup minced onion
3 tablespoons snipped fresh parsley

Pound each side of pork lightly to flatten.

Mix bread cubes, poultry seasoning, thyme, marjoram, sage, celery seeds, pepper and salt in bowl.

Melt butter in saucepan. Add onion and parsley. Simmer until onion is translucent but not browned. Add to dry ingredients and mix well.

Place the stuffing on 1 piece of the pork loin. Top with other half. Secure with string, tying in 4 places along the pork loin. Place in baking pan.

Bake at 350 degrees for $1^1/2$ hours.

Cut into 2-inch slices.

Yield: 2 to 3 servings

MEATS

Honey Bourbon Grilled Pork Tenderloin

3 (12-ounce) pork tenderloins
$1/2$ cup chopped onion
$1/2$ cup lemon juice
$1/2$ cup bourbon
$1/4$ cup honey
$1/4$ cup soy sauce
1 tablespoon minced peeled
gingerroot

4 to 5 cloves of garlic, minced
2 tablespoons olive oil
$1/2$ teaspoon salt
$1/2$ teaspoon pepper
1 to $1^1/4$ cups water or beef or
veal stock
3 tablespoons flour

Trim fat from tenderloins. Combine onion, lemon juice, bourbon, honey, soy sauce, gingerroot, garlic and olive oil in large bowl and mix well. Add pork. Marinate for 30 minutes or longer. Remove pork from marinade, reserving marinade. Sprinkle pork with salt and pepper.

Grill, covered, for 30 minutes or until meat thermometer registers 160 degrees, turning and basting occasionally with reserved marinade.

Combine remaining marinade, water and flour in saucepan, whisking until blended. Bring to a boil over medium heat. Cook for 3 minutes or until thickened.

Serve with tenderloins.

Yield: 9 servings

MEATS

Hunan Pork

1¹/₄ pounds boneless lean pork
2 tablespoons soy sauce
2 tablespoons dry sherry
1 tablespoon brown sugar
2 teaspoons red wine vinegar
1¹/₂ teaspoons sesame oil
¹/₄ teaspoon crushed red
   pepper flakes
¹/₄ teaspoon minced gingerroot
¹/₄ teaspoon dry mustard
1 clove of garlic, minced
1 teaspoon cornstarch
2 tablespoons cold water

1 tablespoon peanut oil
   or vegetable oil
1 small red pepper,
   cut into thin strips
1 small green pepper,
   cut into thin strips
1 clove of garlic, minced
¹/₈ teaspoon crushed red
   pepper flakes
¹/₄ cup chopped scallions
4 teaspoons peanut oil
   or vegetable oil
¹/₃ cup sliced water chestnuts

Trim excess fat from pork; slice pork crossgrain into 1¹/₂-inch strips.

Combine soy sauce, sherry, brown sugar, vinegar, sesame oil, ¹/₄ teaspoon red pepper flakes, gingerroot, dry mustard and 1 clove of garlic in 9x9-inch baking dish and mix well. Add pork, tossing to coat. Marinate, covered, in refrigerator for 2 hours or longer, turning once. Drain marinade into small cup. Stir in cornstarch and cold water and set aside.

Heat 1 tablespoon peanut oil in 10-inch skillet over medium-high heat. Add peppers, 1 clove of garlic and ¹/₈ teaspoon red pepper flakes. Cook for 3 minutes or until peppers and garlic are tender-crisp, stirring constantly. Add scallions. Cook for 1 minute, stirring constantly. Remove vegetables to plate.

Add remaining 4 teaspoons peanut oil to skillet. Add pork strips. Cook for 5 minutes or until cooked through, stirring constantly. Return vegetables to skillet. Add water chestnuts and marinade. Cook for 30 seconds or until thickened and heated through, stirring constantly.

Yield: 6 to 8 servings

MEATS

Chinese Egg Foo Yung with Hot Soy Sauce

1 medium green bell pepper, chopped	1/8 teaspoon pepper, or to taste
1 medium onion, chopped	5 eggs
1 cup chopped pork	2 tablespoons cornstarch
1 (5-ounce) can sliced water chestnuts	1/4 cup cold water
1 cup bean sprouts, drained	2 cups boiling soup stock, bouillon, or consommé
2 to 3 tablespoons soy sauce	2 tablespoons soy sauce

Sauté green pepper and onion in lightly oiled heavy skillet until tender. Add pork. Sauté until cooked through. Stir in water chestnuts, bean sprouts, 2 to 3 tablespoons soy sauce and pepper. Remove from heat.

Beat eggs in bowl for 5 minutes or until thickened. Stir in pork mixture.

Heat lightly oiled skillet over medium heat. Ladle pork mixture with soup ladle or cup into skillet to form patties. Cook until browned, turning once; be careful not to burn eggs. Wrap patties in foil and keep warm.

Make a paste of cornstarch and cold water. Stir into boiling stock in saucepan. Add 2 tablespoons soy sauce. Cook until clear and thickened, stirring constantly. Remove foil from pork patties and place patties on serving platter. Pour hot soy sauce over pork patties.

Yield: 16 servings

MEATS

Pilsen

Pilsen emerged after the Chicago Fire of 1871, when Bohemian immigrants moved west of the city along the south branch of the Chicago River. The influence of these early Czech settlers arriving through this port of entry in the 1890s was so pervasive that Pilsen took its name from Bohemia's second-largest city.

Today, Pilsen continues to serve arriving immigrants, mostly Spanish-speaking families from Mexico. Pilsen and its neighbors, Heart of Chicago and Little Village, form the center of Chicago's flourishing Mexican community.

The brightly painted murals along 18th Street reflect the proud heritage and art of Pilsen's residents. The finest work done by local Latino artists and others from around the country is on display at the Mexican Fine Arts Center. In recent years, many other artists have moved into the area and are thriving in Pilsen.

Decorated door

Mexican Fiesta

Authentic Guacamole 30

Margarita Chicken 174

Black Bean, Corn and Tomato Salad 85

Mexican Corn Bread 56

Margarita Ice Cream Torte 229

POULTRY

Margarita Chicken

Poultry

Chicken Likka

1 pound chicken breasts	$^1/_2$ teaspoon ground allspice or
$^1/_2$ teaspoon salt	garam masala
Juice of $^1/_2$ lemon	$^1/_4$ teaspoon ground nutmeg
1 tablespoon tomato purée	$^1/_2$ teaspoon ground turmeric
2 to 3 cloves of garlic,	$^1/_2$ teaspoon chili powder
peeled, chopped	$^1/_2$ teaspoon salt
1 ($^1/_2$-inch) piece gingerroot,	5 ounces thick-set natural yogurt or
chopped	regular yogurt
2 teaspoons ground coriander	$^1/_4$ cup vegetable oil

Rinse chicken and pat dry. Cut into 1-inch pieces; place in large bowl. Sprinkle with $^1/_2$ teaspoon salt and lemon juice. Marinate, covered, for 30 minutes.

Combine tomato purée, garlic, gingerroot, coriander, allspice, nutmeg, turmeric, chili powder, $^1/_2$ teaspoon salt, yogurt and oil in food processor container. Process until smooth. Mix with chicken.

Marinate, covered, in refrigerator for 6 to 8 hours.

Remove chicken from marinade, reserving marinade. Thread chicken pieces $^1/_4$ inch apart onto skewers. Place in foil-lined baking pan. Coat with part of the reserved marinade.

Bake in center section of oven at 450 degrees for 6 to 8 minutes. Turn skewers. Coat with remaining marinade. Bake for 6 to 8 minutes or until chicken is cooked through.

Serve on or off skewers.

Yield: 4 servings

POULTRY

Oven-Fried Chicken

Contributed by Governor and Mrs. Jim Edgar.

2 skinless chicken breasts
1 cup skim milk
2 egg whites
1 tablespoon fresh parsley
1 teaspoon tarragon
1 clove of garlic, minced
2 teaspoons Worcestershire sauce
$^1/_8$ teaspoon pepper, or to taste
$^1/_3$ cup plain nonfat yogurt
$^1/_4$ cup crushed cornflakes
2 tablespoons cornmeal

Rinse chicken. Soak in milk in large bowl.

Mix egg whites, parsley, tarragon, garlic, Worcestershire sauce, pepper and yogurt in medium bowl.

Remove chicken from milk. Brush with yogurt mixture. Roll in cornflakes. Dust with cornmeal. Place in baking dish sprayed with nonstick cooking spray.

Bake at 375 degrees for 45 to 55 minutes or until chicken is cooked through.

Serve with Peppery Chicken Pan Gravy.

Yield: 2 to 3 servings

Peppery Chicken Pan Gravy

2 tablespoons flour
2 cups skim milk
1 tablespoon chicken base
$^1/_2$ teaspoon poultry seasoning
1 teaspoon pepper
1 teaspoon lemon juice
1 tablespoon browned breading from Oven-Fried Chicken

Combine flour and skim milk in container with cover. Shake, covered, for 1 minute or until all lumps are dissolved.

Pour into saucepan. Bring to a boil. Cook until thickened, stirring constantly.

Add chicken base, poultry seasoning, pepper and lemon juice. Cook just until thickened.

Stir in breading.

Serve with Oven-Fried Chicken.

Yield: 2 to 3 servings

POULTRY

Tandoori Chicken

1 (2-inch) piece fresh gingerroot, peeled, grated
4 cloves of garlic, peeled, grated
1 teaspoon cumin seeds
$^1/_2$ teaspoon cayenne
$^1/_4$ teaspoon salt
1 cup plain yogurt
1 (4-pound) chicken, cut up
2 tablespoons vegetable oil
$^1/_2$ teaspoon turmeric

Mix gingerroot, garlic, cumin seeds, cayenne, salt and yogurt in bowl.

Rinse chicken and pat dry. Place on foil-lined baking pan. Pour yogurt mixture over chicken, spreading to coat completely. Marinate in refrigerator for 2 hours to overnight.

Drizzle oil over chicken. Sprinkle with turmeric.

Bake at 350 degrees for 1 hour, basting frequently with oil and yogurt marinade from bottom of pan.

Serve with hot pita bread .

Yield: 4 servings

Chicken Breasts with Lemon Sauce

4 boneless skinless chicken breasts,
cut into halves horizontally
$^1/_2$ cup flour
$^1/_4$ cup margarine
2 cloves of garlic, chopped
1 cup dry white wine
2 tablespoons lemon juice
$^1/_2$ teaspoon freshly ground pepper

Rinse chicken and pat dry. Dredge chicken with flour.

Heat margarine in skillet over medium-high heat. Add chicken and garlic. Cook for 5 minutes or until browned, turning once. Add wine and lemon juice. Sprinkle with pepper. Cook until chicken is cooked through.

Yield: 4 to 6 servings

Chicken Breasts Veronique

3 whole chicken breasts
$^1/_4$ cup flour
$^1/_2$ teaspoon salt
$^1/_4$ teaspoon pepper
$^1/_4$ teaspoon tarragon
$^1/_4$ cup butter
$^1/_4$ cup chopped onion
$^1/_2$ cup dry white wine
$^1/_2$ cup chicken stock
8 ounces fresh mushrooms, sliced
3 tablespoons butter
2 cups seedless grapes, cut into halves

Debone and skin chicken; cut into halves. Rinse and pat dry. Coat in mixture of flour, salt, pepper and tarragon. Brown in $^1/_4$ cup butter in skillet, adding additional butter if needed. Arrange chicken in single layer in baking dish.

Add onion to skillet. Sauté gently. Add wine and chicken stock. Bring to a gentle boil. Pour over chicken.

Bake, covered with foil, at 375 degrees for 45 minutes.

Sauté mushrooms gently in 3 tablespoons butter in skillet.

Add grapes. Sauté for 5 minutes. Pour over chicken.

Bake, uncovered, for 10 minutes longer.

Yield: 6 servings

Margarita Chicken

2 tablespoons finely chopped poblano chile, or
1 teaspoon minced jalapeño
4 teaspoons tequila
1 tablespoon corn oil
1 tablespoon fresh lime juice
2 teaspoons chopped fresh parsley
1 teaspoon grated lime peel
1 teaspoon chopped fresh tarragon, or
$^1/_4$ teaspoon dried
1 teaspoon honey
$^1/_2$ teaspoon salt
Freshly ground pepper to taste
4 (4-ounce) boneless skinless chicken breasts

Mix chile, tequila, corn oil, lime juice, parsley, lime peel, tarragon, honey, salt and pepper in bowl.

Rinse chicken and pat dry. Arrange in single layer in shallow baking dish. Pour tequila mixture over chicken. Chill, covered, for 8 to 10 hours.

Remove chicken from marinade. Pour remaining marinade into small heavy saucepan and set aside.

Wrap each chicken breast in foil. Place on large heavy baking sheet.

Bake at 450 degrees for 15 minutes or until cooked through. Let stand at room temperature for 10 minutes. Remove chicken from foil. Slice and fan on plates.

Bring reserved marinade to a boil. Pour over chicken.

Yield: 4 servings

POULTRY

Sesame Chicken

$^1/_4$ cup soy sauce
2 tablespoons honey
1 tablespoon dry white wine
1 teaspoon ginger
2 cloves of garlic, minced
4 boneless skinless chicken breasts
$^1/_2$ cup flour
$^1/_2$ cup sesame seeds
2 egg whites, beaten
2 tablespoons butter
2 tablespoons olive oil

Whisk soy sauce, honey, wine, ginger and garlic in large bowl.

Rinse chicken and pat dry. Add to soy sauce mixture. Marinate, covered, in refrigerator for 8 to 10 hours.

Heat large cast-iron skillet in 500-degree oven.

Remove chicken from marinade. Mix flour and sesame seeds in sealable plastic bag.

Dip chicken in egg whites. Shake in flour mixture until coated.

Add butter and olive oil to hot skillet. Add chicken in single layer, turning to coat well.

Bake at 500 degrees for 5 to 10 minutes or until chicken is cooked through.

Yield: 4 servings

Stuffed Chicken

8 small boneless skinless chicken breasts
1 onion, chopped
2 tablespoons margarine
1 (10-ounce) package frozen chopped broccoli, thawed
2 cups shredded Swiss cheese

Rinse chicken and pat dry. Pound chicken thin.

Sauté onion in margarine in skillet. Stir in broccoli.

Remove from heat. Stir in cheese. Place 1 spoonful on each piece of chicken. Fold in sides and roll up. Place in baking dish. Top with remaining broccoli mixture.

Bake at 325 degrees for 25 minutes or until chicken is cooked through.

Yield: 8 servings

POULTRY

Zesty Chicken Cacciatore

1 (6-ounce) can tomato paste
$^1/_2$ cup olive oil
$^1/_4$ cup natural-flavored raspberry
aged red wine vinegar
$^1/_3$ cup cabernet sauvignon
$^1/_2$ teaspoon cayenne
$^1/_4$ teaspoon red pepper flakes

$^1/_2$ teaspoon salt
$^1/_2$ teaspoon freshly ground black
pepper
1 teaspoon Paul Prudhomme's
seasoning
4 boneless skinless chicken breasts

Combine tomato paste, olive oil, vinegar, wine, cayenne, red pepper flakes, salt, black pepper and seasoning in large bowl and mix well.

Rinse chicken and pat dry. Arrange in large shallow baking dish. Pour marinade over chicken. Marinate in refrigerator for 1 hour to overnight.

Prepare hot grill with coals and a fragrant wood such as mesquite or hickory.

Remove chicken from marinade, reserving marinade. Grill or broil for 8 to 10 minutes per side or until cooked through, basting occasionally with reserved marinade.

Season to taste. Serve with side dish of pasta.

Yield: 4 servings

POULTRY

A Mexican bakery in Pilsen

Chicken Fajitas

3 whole chicken breasts
1 large green bell pepper, chopped
1 large onion, thinly sliced
2 tablespoons oregano
1 teaspoon pepper

$^1/_4$ cup lemon juice
$^1/_2$ cup olive oil
$^1/_4$ cup margarine
1 to 2 teaspoons liquid smoke
Tabasco sauce to taste

Debone chicken and remove skin; cut into halves. Rinse and pat dry.

Combine chicken, green pepper and onion in glass casserole. Sprinkle with oregano and pepper. Add lemon juice and olive oil. Marinate in refrigerator for 2 hours.

Bake, covered with foil, at 350 degrees for 30 minutes or until chicken is thoroughly white. Remove to platter to cool; reserve marinade. Pull or cut chicken into 1-inch pieces.

Heat margarine in heavy skillet over medium-high heat. Add chicken. Sprinkle with liquid smoke. Cook until chicken is browned, stirring frequently. Add green pepper and onion from marinade. Cook until lightly browned. Stir in remaining marinade. Stir in Tabasco sauce. Simmer, covered, over medium heat for 10 to 20 minutes or until chicken is cooked through.

Remove chicken to large platter. Serve with chopped tomatoes, guacamole, tomato salsa and sour cream as toppings. Serve with side dishes of refried beans and warm tortillas.

Yield: 8 servings

POULTRY

Chicken and Wild Mushroom Strudel with Dried Cherries

$^{1}/_{4}$ cup butter
$^{1}/_{4}$ cup flour
2 cups chicken stock
$^{1}/_{2}$ cup whipping cream
1 teaspoon crushed fresh
rosemary or sage
2 cups chopped cooked chicken

$^{1}/_{2}$ cup chopped wild mushrooms
$^{1}/_{2}$ cup dried Michigan cherries
1 package phyllo dough, thawed
$^{1}/_{2}$ cup melted butter
Sour cream (optional)
Sprigs of fresh rosemary

Combine $^{1}/_{4}$ cup butter and flour in saucepan. Cook over low heat for 5 minutes or until smooth, stirring constantly.

Add chicken stock, whipping cream and rosemary. Simmer for 10 minutes or longer.

Add chicken, mushrooms and cherries. Cook until heated through.

Working with 3 sheets of phyllo at a time, brush each sheet with melted butter and layer one over the other. Spread a 1x2-inch layer of chicken mixture over dough approximately 3 inches from left side, leaving $1^{1}/_{2}$ inches at each end of dough. Fold dough from top and sides like an envelope over filling. Roll into a log, brushing lightly with melted butter to seal as needed. Repeat procedure with remaining dough and chicken mixture. Place in baking pan.

Bake at 350 degrees for 15 to 20 minutes or until golden brown. Top each serving with dollop of sour cream and sprig of rosemary. Serve immediately.

Yield: 6 to 8 servings

POULTRY

Sautéed Chicken with Artichokes and Tarragon Cream Sauce

$^1/_2$ cup red wine vinegar
2 teaspoons dried tarragon
1 teaspoon minced shallots
Pepper to taste
$^1/_2$ cup flour
Salt to taste
1 pound boneless skinless
chicken breasts, cut into
$^3/_4$-inch strips

2 tablespoons vegetable oil
2 cups sliced mushrooms
1 cup dry white wine
1 cup low-sodium chicken broth
2 teaspoons minced shallots
1 cup whipping cream
8 canned artichoke hearts,
rinsed, drained, cut into quarters

Combine vinegar, tarragon, 1 teaspoon shallots and pepper in small saucepan. Boil until most of liquid has evaporated.

Mix flour, salt and additional pepper in shallow bowl. Rinse chicken and pat dry. Coat chicken with flour mixture, shaking off excess.

Heat oil in large skillet over medium-high heat until hot but not smoking. Add chicken. Sauté for 1 minute.

Add mushrooms, wine, chicken broth, tarragon mixture and 2 teaspoons shallots. Cook until chicken is no longer pink and cooked through, stirring occasionally. Remove chicken to platter with slotted spoon.

Boil cooking liquids until reduced by $^2/_3$, stirring occasionally. Stir in whipping cream and artichoke hearts. Boil until of desired consistency, stirring occasionally. Pour over chicken.

Yield: 4 servings

POULTRY

Paella

2 to 4 cups chicken stock
$^1/_4$ gram saffron threads
1 pound boneless skinless chicken breasts
$^1/_4$ cup olive oil
8 ounces spicy sausage, cut into bite-size pieces
1 (12-ounce) can tomatoes
$^1/_2$ red bell pepper, chopped
1 cup arborio rice
$^1/_4$ cup peas
$1^1/_2$ pounds prawns, shelled
Salt and pepper to taste

Heat chicken stock in medium saucepan. Add saffron. Turn off heat; allow to steep.

Rinse chicken and pat dry. Cut into bite-size pieces. Sauté in olive oil in 13-inch paella pan over medium heat until golden brown. Drain on paper towels.

Add sausage to paella pan. Cook until browned. Drain on paper towels.

Add undrained tomatoes, red pepper, rice and chicken to pan. Add enough saffron liquid to cover rice. Simmer for 20 minutes or until cooked through.

Add sausage, peas and prawns and mix gently, adding additional saffron liquid if needed. Season with salt and pepper.

Serve directly from paella pan.

Yield: 4 servings

Oriental Dipping Sauce for Poultry

1 teaspoon chili paste with garlic
$^1/_2$ tablespoon chopped fresh gingerroot
$^1/_4$ cup tamari
$^1/_2$ tablespoon Oriental sesame oil
$1^1/_2$ tablespoons freshly squeezed lemon juice
$1^1/_2$ tablespoons sake

Combine chili paste and gingerroot in small bowl. Stir in tamari gradually. Stir in sesame oil, lemon juice and sake.

Let stand at room temperature for 1 hour. Stir before serving.

May also be served with fish.

Yield: $^3/_4$ cup

Harry Caray's Chicken

Chef Abraham Aguirre serves this recipe at Harry Caray's Restaurant.

1/2 chicken
1/2 teaspoon salt
1/2 teaspoon pepper
2 teaspoons oregano
2 teaspoons granulated garlic
1 large potato, peeled, quartered
6 tablespoons olive oil
2 large cloves of garlic
1/2 cup dry white wine
2 ounces frozen peas, blanched
2 teaspoons chopped parsley

Rinse chicken and pat dry. Cut chicken into 4 pieces. Season with salt, pepper, oregano and granulated garlic.

Sauté potato in olive oil in 10-inch ovenproof skillet until golden brown. Remove potato and set aside. Heat olive oil in skillet to 300 degrees. Add garlic. Sauté for 2 minutes. Add chicken. Sauté until golden brown. Return potato to skillet. Add wine, stirring to deglaze skillet.

Bake at 400 degrees for 20 to 30 minutes.

Place chicken on serving plate. Arrange potato around chicken. Pour sauce from skillet over chicken. Add peas. Sprinkle with parsley.

Yield: 2 servings

Polynesian Turkey

1 (20-ounce) can syrup-pack pineapple chunks
3 (6-ounce) cans frozen pineapple juice
1/4 cup soy sauce
1 teaspoon salt
1/4 teaspoon powdered ginger
1/4 teaspoon garlic powder
3 cups chopped cooked turkey
5 to 6 tablespoons cornstarch
1 (8-ounce) can pitted medium olives
1 large green bell pepper, cut into 1-inch pieces
1 (4-ounce) jar pimentos, drained
Buttered rice

Drain pineapple, reserving syrup.

Combine reserved syrup, pineapple juice, soy sauce, salt, ginger and garlic powder in large bowl and mix well. Add turkey. Marinate for 1 hour.

Drain marinade into large skillet. Blend in cornstarch. Heat slowly until mixture boils and thickens, stirring constantly.

Add olives, green pepper, pimentos, pineapple and turkey. Simmer, covered, for 5 to 10 minutes or until heated through.

Serve over buttered rice.

Yield: 6 to 8 servings

Black Bean Turkey Chili

1 package black beans
4 to 5 cups water
2 (28-ounce) cans crushed tomatoes in purée
1 medium can tomato paste
2 pounds ground turkey
2 to 3 yellow onions, chopped
1 to 2 red bell peppers, chopped
1 to 2 green bell peppers, chopped
2 to 3 tablespoons cumin
2 to 3 tablespoons cayenne
2 to 3 tablespoons chili powder
2 tablespoons hot sauce
1 small can chopped green chiles (optional)

Rinse and sort beans. Soak in water to cover overnight; drain and rinse. Combine beans, 4 to 5 cups water, tomatoes and tomato paste in large deep crock or pan. Simmer gently.

Brown turkey in skillet; drain well. Return turkey to skillet. Add half the onion and half the bell peppers. Stir in half the cumin, cayenne and chili powder. Cook for 10 minutes.

Add turkey mixture to beans and mix well. Bring to a boil; return to a simmer. Add remaining onions, bell peppers, cumin, cayenne and chili powder. Add hot sauce and green chiles. Simmer, covered, for 2 hours, stirring occasionally. Simmer, uncovered, for 2 hours, stirring occasionally. Adjust seasonings.

May top each serving with chopped onion, shredded Cheddar cheese and sour cream.

Yield: 12 to 14 servings

Thai Turkey Burgers

1³/₄ pounds ground turkey
2 teaspoons black bean sauce
1 teaspoon minced garlic
1 teaspoon minced ginger
1 small jalapeño, minced
¹/₂ teaspoon cayenne
¹/₄ cup chopped cilantro
1 teaspoon hoisin sauce
¹/₂ cup bread crumbs
1 egg white
1 tablespoon sherry (optional)
Salt and pepper to taste

Combine turkey, black bean sauce, garlic, ginger, jalapeño, cayenne, cilantro, hoisin sauce, bread crumbs, egg white and sherry in bowl and mix well. Season with salt and pepper. Shape into patties.

Grill briefly over high heat; reduce heat to medium. Turn patties when grill marks appear. Grill for 8 to 14 minutes or until cooked through.

Yield: 4 servings

POULTRY

Bridgeport

Bridgeport, one of the most famous neighbor-hoods in the city, predates the founding of the Union Stockyards. Irish workers came to dig the Illinois-Michigan Canal and settled along the river in this area, known originally as Lee's Farm. The name Bridgeport was coined from the building of the canal. Later, meat-packing plants opened along the South Branch of the Chicago River. These plants drew more Irish workers, as well as skilled German and Bohemian butchers, to Bridgeport. On Christmas Day, 1865, the Union Stockyards opened just south of Bridgeport, forging Chicago's fame as the leader in livestock trading and meat-packing.

Much of the area's notoriety arises from its working class ethnicity and its political offspring. Richard J. Daley, its best-known son, was one of four Chicago mayors born and raised in Bridgeport; those four collectively ran the city from 1933 until 1979. Today, visitors to Bridgeport will find a strong Latino-based community surrounding the home of the Chicago White Sox.

The original gate to the Union Stockyards

Celebration of Ireland

Curried Zucchini and Potato Soup 68

Ginger-Mustard Salmon with Lemon Sauce 190

Steamed Asparagus

Irish Soda Bread 55

Pine Nut Brown Sugar Shortbread 215

Ginger-Mustard Salmon with Lemon Sauce

Seafood

Red Snapper with Tomato Sauce

6 fresh red snapper fillets
Salt and pepper to taste
$1/4$ to $1/2$ cup flour
$1/4$ cup olive oil
3 large shallots, minced
3 large cloves of garlic,
finely chopped
6 to 8 tomatoes, peeled,
seeded, chopped
2 tablespoons finely chopped mixed
fresh oregano, thyme and chervil, or
2 teaspoons dried

1 ripe avocado
1 to 2 teaspoons lime juice
$1/8$ teaspoon hot pepper sauce,
or to taste
1 tablespoon tomato paste
(optional)
Avocado slices
Lime slices

Season fish with salt and pepper. Dredge in flour, shaking to remove excess.

Heat olive oil in large skillet. Add fish. Sauté for 2 minutes per side. Remove to ovenproof baking dish.

Sauté shallots and garlic in same skillet until lightly browned. Add tomatoes. Cook for 3 to 4 minutes or until heated through. Pour over fish. Sprinkle with herbs.

Bake, covered with buttered waxed paper, at 350 degrees for 25 to 30 minutes or until cooked through.

Mash 1 avocado in small bowl. Add lime juice, additional salt and pepper and hot pepper sauce.

Lift fish carefully from baking dish and place on warm platter. Place baking dish over direct heat. Cook until pan drippings are reduced by $1/3$. Add tomato paste. Reduce heat. Add avocado mixture; do not boil. Adjust seasonings. Pour over fish.

Top with avocado and lime slices.

Yield: 6 servings

SEAFOOD

Ginger-Mustard Salmon with Lemon Sauce

This recipe was contributed by The Chicago Tribune.

1 (1-inch) piece of fresh
ginger, peeled
1 teaspoon grated lemon peel
3 tablespoons fresh lemon juice
2 tablespoons vegetable oil
2 tablespoons honey
2 teaspoons grainy mustard
2 teaspoons soy sauce
$^{1}/_{2}$ teaspoon salt
4 (6- to 7-pound) salmon fillets
1 tablespoon vegetable oil

$^{1}/_{2}$ cup dry white wine
1 tablespoon seasoned or
plain rice vinegar
1 large shallot, minced
1 teaspoon dried rosemary
3 tablespoons whipping cream
2 tablespoons unsalted butter
Salt and freshly ground white
pepper to taste
Fresh chives

Process ginger and lemon peel in food processor until minced. Add lemon juice, 2 tablespoons oil, honey, mustard, soy sauce and $^{1}/_{2}$ teaspoon salt; mix well. Reserve half the marinade for sauce. Pour remaining marinade in sealable plastic food storage bag. Add salmon; seal bag. Marinate in refrigerator for 30 minutes or for up to 8 hours.

Heat 1 tablespoon oil in cast-iron skillet over high heat. Drain salmon. Add salmon to skillet skin side down. Cook for 3 minutes. Remove skillet to oven. Bake at 450 degrees for 5 to 6 minutes or until cooked through.

Combine wine, rice vinegar, shallot and rosemary in small nonaluminum saucepan. Bring to a boil over high heat. Boil for 6 to 8 minutes or until mixture is reduced to 3 tablespoons. Add reserved marinade and cream. Cook until reduced to 6 tablespoons. Reduce heat to low. Cut butter into 2 pieces. Whisk 1 piece of butter at a time into sauce until melted. Stir in salt and white pepper to taste.

Place salmon on individual serving plates. Garnish with chives. Strain sauce into bowl and serve with salmon.

Yield: 4 servings

SEAFOOD

Grilled Salmon in Cabernet Sauvignon Sauce

1¹/₂ teaspoons minced shallots
1¹/₄ cups cabernet sauvignon
¹/₄ cup tarragon vinegar
¹/₂ cup unsalted butter, softened,
cut into 8 pieces
Salt and pepper to taste
Olive oil
4 (6- to 7-ounce) salmon fillets

Sauté shallots in nonreactive pan until translucent. Add wine and vinegar. Boil until reduced by ³/₄. Strain out shallots. Return liquid to pan.

Whisk in butter 1 piece at a time over low heat. Season with salt and pepper.

Sprinkle olive oil over salmon. Grill on rack in preheated broiler until almost done. Finish cooking in 350-degree oven for 3 to 4 minutes or until salmon is light pink and flakes easily.

Serve immediately with wine sauce.

Yield: 4 servings

Baked Sole with Light Sauce

5 tablespoons margarine
¹/₈ teaspoon garlic
2 tablespoons flour
¹/₄ teaspoon paprika, or to taste
¹/₈ teaspoon white pepper, or to taste
¹/₂ cup chicken broth
¹/₂ cup skim milk
2 teaspoons fresh lemon juice
1¹/₂ pounds sole
1 tablespoon margarine

Melt 5 tablespoons margarine in medium saucepan over medium heat. Add garlic. Cook for 30 seconds, stirring constantly.

Stir in flour, paprika and pepper. Cook for 1 minute, stirring constantly.

Whisk in chicken broth, skim milk and lemon juice gradually. Cook for 2 minutes or until thickened, stirring constantly. Keep warm.

Place sole in greased baking pan. Dot with 1 tablespoon margarine.

Bake at 350 degrees for 10 minutes.

Remove fish to platter. Pour sauce over fish. Sprinkle with additional paprika.

Serve with steamed broccoli and angel hair pasta topped with butter and Parmesan cheese for a quick midweek dinner.

Yield: 2 servings

SEAFOOD

Zuppa di Pesce

2 tablespoons olive oil
1 large clove of garlic, crushed
4 ounces swordfish
4 ounces calamari
2 small clams
2 shrimp, peeled, deveined
8 mussels
$^{1}/_{8}$ teaspoon oregano, or to taste
1 bay leaf
Salt and pepper to taste
$^{1}/_{2}$ cup tomato sauce
2 tablespoons red wine

Heat olive oil in large saucepan over medium heat. Add garlic. Cook until browned; do not burn.

Add swordfish, calamari, clams, shrimp, mussels, oregano, bay leaf, salt, pepper, tomato sauce and wine and mix gently. Cook for 5 minutes or until clams open. Remove bay leaf.

Serve over linguini.

Yield: 1 serving

Swordfish with Gingered Mango Sauce

2 tablespoons margarine
6 tablespoons chopped shallots
2 tablespoons chopped ginger
1 tablespoon chopped garlic
1 cup dry white wine
2 mangoes, peeled, seeded
1 cup fish stock
2 tablespoons half-and-half
$^{1}/_{4}$ cup freshly squeezed lime juice
6 (8-ounce) swordfish steaks
Salt and pepper to taste
Olive oil
$^{1}/_{4}$ cup chopped fresh mint

Melt margarine in saucepan over medium heat. Add shallots, ginger and garlic. Sauté until tender.

Add wine. Cook until liquid is reduced to $^{1}/_{4}$ cup.

Combine garlic mixture, mangoes and fish stock in food processor container. Process until puréed. Add to saucepan.

Add half-and-half and lime juice. Cook over medium heat for 8 to 10 minutes or until heated through. Set aside and keep warm.

Season swordfish lightly with salt and pepper. Brush with olive oil. Grill over high heat for 5 to 8 minutes per side or until fish flakes easily.

Stir mint into sauce. Drizzle 2 tablespoons sauce over each steak.

Yield: 6 servings

Tilapia with Lemon Caper Butter

$^1/_2$ cup unsalted butter, softened
$^1/_4$ cup capers, rinsed, drained
$^1/_8$ teaspoon ground white pepper, or to taste
1 teaspoon grated lemon zest
$^1/_4$ teaspoon fresh lemon juice
4 (6-ounce) fresh tilapia fillets
$^1/_4$ cup flour
2 tablespoons olive oil

Mix butter, capers, pepper, lemon zest and lemon juice with fork in small bowl; do not use blender or food processor. Place mixture in center of 8x8-inch piece of baking parchment, leaving at least $1^1/_2$-inch margin on all sides. Overlap 2 opposing sides of parchment to roll butter mixture into log or cylinder; parchment edges will stick to each other to hold log in place. Twist 2 long ends of parchment to seal. Place in freezer until firm.

Rinse fish and pat dry. Dredge in flour. Heat olive oil in 10-inch skillet over medium-high heat. Add fish. Sauté for 3 minutes per side. Drain on paper towels; remove to warm platter.

Remove paper from butter log. Slice into $^1/_4$-inch rounds. Place 1 round over each fillet to melt.

Serve with baked potatoes and a green vegetable.

Tilapia, a member of the perch family, has a flavor and texture similar to other freshwater lake fish.

Yield: 4 servings

Crab Imperial

1 egg, beaten
2 tablespoons mayonnaise
2 teaspoons flour
1 teaspoon parsley
$^1/_4$ teaspoon dry mustard
$^1/_8$ teaspoon Worcestershire sauce, or to taste
Salt and pepper to taste
1 pound fresh crab meat, deboned, flaked
2 egg yolks, slightly beaten
1 tablespoon melted butter
1 tablespoon mayonnaise
Paprika to taste

Blend egg, 2 tablespoons mayonnaise, flour, parsley, dry mustard, Worcestershire sauce, salt and pepper in medium bowl.

Pour over crab meat in large bowl; mix lightly. Spoon into shell ramekins.

Mix egg yolks, butter, 1 tablespoon mayonnaise and additional salt in medium bowl. Pour over crab meat. Sprinkle with paprika.

Bake at 375 degrees for 12 to 15 minutes or until lightly browned.

Yield: 4 servings

SEAFOOD

Grilled Crab Burgers

6 ounces fresh crab meat, or
1 (6-ounce) can, drained
1 cup fresh Italian bread crumbs
$^1/_2$ cup chopped green onions
2 tablespoons mayonnaise
1 teaspoon Old Bay seasoning
Salt and pepper to taste
1 egg yolk
$^1/_2$ cup fresh Italian bread crumbs
4 large slices French bread
$2^1/_2$ tablespoons mayonnaise
$1^1/_2$ tablespoons Dijon mustard

Mix crab meat, 1 cup bread crumbs, green onions,
2 tablespoons mayonnaise, seasoning, salt and
pepper in medium bowl. Stir in egg yolk. Shape into
four $2^1/_2$-inch patties. Dip in remaining $^1/_2$ cup
bread crumbs, turning to coat completely.

Grill on oiled rack over medium-high heat for 4
minutes per side or until golden brown. Grill bread
slices for 1 minute per side or until lightly toasted.

Spread toast with mixture of $2^1/_2$ tablespoons
mayonnaise and Dijon mustard. Top with burgers.

Recipe may be doubled.

Yield: 2 servings

Scallops with Asian Sauce

$1^1/_2$ pounds scallops
1 tablespoon wine
2 tablespoons vegetable oil
1 large clove of garlic, finely chopped
2 tablespoons rinsed black beans, chopped
2 scallions, coarsely chopped
4 ounces ground pork
1 tablespoon dark soy sauce
Salt and pepper to taste
$^1/_4$ teaspoon sugar
1 cup plus 3 tablespoons fish stock
2 tablespoons cornstarch
2 eggs, slightly beaten

Stir-fry scallops in nonstick skillet over high heat
for 2 to 3 minutes. Add wine. Stir-fry for 30 seconds.
Remove scallops to bowl; drain skillet.

Heat oil in skillet. Add garlic, beans and scallions.
Stir-fry for 30 seconds. Add pork. Cook until pork
is cooked through.

Add soy sauce, salt, pepper, sugar and fish stock.
Cover and bring to a boil. Stir in cornstarch.

Add eggs gradually, stirring until scrambled. Stir
in scallops.

Serve with rice.

Yield: 6 servings

SEAFOOD

Shrimp Curry

1 cup chopped carrots
1 cup chopped celery
1 large onion, chopped
1 large Red Delicious apple or Granny Smith
apple, peeled, chopped
1 large green, yellow or red bell pepper, chopped
$2^3/_4$ cups dry white wine
1 (14-ounce) can tomatoes, crushed
$^1/_4$ cup dry white wine
2 tablespoons curry powder
4 servings cooked shrimp
4 servings cooked couscous or rice
Chutney to taste

Combine carrots, celery, onion, apple, green
pepper and $2^3/_4$ cups wine in 10-inch skillet. Simmer
for 30 minutes.

Add undrained tomatoes. Stir in mixture of $^1/_4$
cup wine and curry powder. Simmer for 30
minutes longer.

Mash mixture in skillet. Simmer, covered, for 30
minutes, adding additional wine if needed.

Stir in shrimp. Cook until heated through.

Divide couscous or rice among 4 plates. Top with
curry. Serve chutney as condiment.

Yield: 4 servings

Jambalaya

1 cup chopped onion
1 cup chopped celery
1 green bell pepper, chopped
2 cloves of garlic, minced
Vegetable oil
1 (16-ounce) can tomatoes
1 (16-ounce) can tomato sauce
Salt and black pepper to taste
$^1/_2$ teaspoon cayenne, or to taste
1 pound sweet Italian sausage, cut into
bite-size pieces
2 pounds shrimp, peeled
4 to 5 cups rice, cooked

Sauté onion, celery, green pepper and garlic in oil
in large saucepan until tender.

Add undrained tomatoes and tomato sauce.
Season with salt, black pepper and cayenne. Simmer
for 1 hour.

Brown sausage in skillet. Stir sausage into hot
mixture.

Add shrimp. Simmer until heated through.

Stir in rice at serving time. Adjust seasonings.

Yield: 8 servings

SEAFOOD

Greek Shrimp

$^{1}/_{4}$ cup olive oil
3 cloves of garlic, chopped
1$^{1}/_{2}$ pounds chopped canned plum tomatoes
Salt and black pepper to taste
1 teaspoon crushed red pepper
$^{1}/_{4}$ cup fish broth or bottled clam juice
1$^{1}/_{2}$ teaspoons dried oregano
2 tablespoons small capers, drained
$^{1}/_{4}$ cup ouzo
$^{1}/_{4}$ cup butter
1$^{1}/_{2}$ pounds large shrimp, peeled
4 teaspoons butter
$^{1}/_{2}$ cup crumbled feta cheese

Heat olive oil in large saucepan. Add garlic. Sauté over medium heat for 1 minute.

Add tomatoes, salt, black pepper and red pepper. Simmer until tomatoes are reduced by $^{1}/_{2}$.

Add fish broth, oregano, capers and ouzo. Simmer for 10 minutes.

Heat $^{1}/_{4}$ cup butter in skillet. Add shrimp. Cook until pink, turning frequently.

Spray 4 shallow ovenproof bowls with nonstick cooking spray. Spoon enough tomato sauce into each to cover bottom. Add 1 teaspoon butter to each bowl. Top with shrimp. Sprinkle with cheese.

Bake at 450 degrees for 10 minutes or until cheese begins to bubble.

Serve with crusty bread.

May serve on bed of sautéed spinach or Swiss chard instead of in bowls.

Yield: 4 servings

Seafood Suprême

$^{1}/_{2}$ cup butter
1 clove of garlic, minced
1 shallot, minced
8 jumbo shrimp
1 pound bay scallops or large sea scallops, cut into quarters
8 ounces white crab meat
1 tablespoon chopped parsley
1 cup Vouvray or other white wine
1 cup whipping cream
Paprika to taste

Melt butter in heavy skillet. Add garlic and shallot. Cook for 1 minute, stirring constantly.

Add shrimp and scallops. Cook for several minutes or until heated through; do not overcook.

Stir in crab meat. Cook for 1 minute, stirring constantly.

Add parsley, wine and whipping cream, stirring after each addition. Adjust seasonings.

Ladle into shallow soup dishes. Sprinkle with paprika.

Serve with French bread.

Yield: 6 to 8 servings

SEAFOOD

Seafood Gumbo

8 ounces Cajun sausage or kielbasa,
cut into $^1/_2$-inch slices
2 tablespoons olive oil
1 pound okra, sliced
2 tablespoons olive oil
2 cups chopped sweet yellow onions
1 cup chopped red bell pepper
1 cup chopped green bell pepper
4 cloves of garlic, crushed
1 teaspoon gumbo filé (optional)
5 cups chicken broth
3 cups crushed fresh or
canned tomatoes

$^1/_2$ teaspoon cayenne
$^1/_3$ teaspoon freshly ground
black pepper
1 bay leaf
1 tablespoon Tabasco sauce
1 pound large or medium shrimp,
peeled, deveined
1 pound sea scallops
8 ounces oysters
8 ounces lump crab meat
$2^1/_2$ tablespoons chopped
fresh parsley
8 servings cooked white rice

Sauté sausage in cast-iron skillet over medium heat for 15 minutes or until browned and slightly crisp. Drain on paper towels.

Heat 2 tablespoons olive oil in large pot. Add okra. Sauté over medium heat for 20 minutes or until tender.

Add 2 tablespoons olive oil, onions, bell peppers and garlic. Cook for 15 minutes.

Add sausage, chicken broth, tomatoes, cayenne, black pepper, bay leaf and Tabasco sauce. Simmer for 30 minutes.

Add shrimp and scallops. Simmer for 5 minutes.

Add oysters, crab meat and parsley. Simmer for 10 minutes or until edges of oysters are curled or rippled. Remove bay leaf.

Serve immediately over rice. Season with additional Tabasco sauce and black pepper.

Yield: 8 servings

SEAFOOD

Mandarin Lobster Club Sandwiches

2 ounces thinly sliced pancetta
1 tablespoon honey
$^{1}/_{2}$ tablespoon vegetable oil
1 cup chopped cooked lobster
$^{1}/_{2}$ cup chopped mango
$^{1}/_{4}$ cup chopped peeled cucumber
2 tablespoons mayonnaise
Salt and pepper to taste

1 cup thinly sliced iceberg lettuce
4 ounces oil-pack sun-dried
tomatoes, cut into thin strips
8 fresh basil leaves,
cut into thin strips
6 slices firm whole wheat sandwich
bread, toasted
Mayonnaise to taste

Brush pancetta with honey. Heat oil in cast-iron skillet over medium-high heat until hot but not smoking. Add pancetta. Cook until crisp. Drain on paper towels.

Combine lobster, mango, cucumber, mayonnaise, salt and pepper in large bowl and mix well.

Combine lettuce, tomatoes and basil in medium bowl and mix gently.

Spread each toast slice with a small amount of additional mayonnaise.

Layer 1 toast slice, half the lobster mixture, 1 toast slice, half the lettuce mixture, half the pancetta and 1 toast slice to make a sandwich. Repeat with remaining ingredients.

Cut each sandwich into halves with serrated knife.

Yield: 2 servings

SEAFOOD

Southern-Style Shrimp

³/₄ cup butter
1 bay leaf
¹/₄ cup fresh lemon juice
1 teaspoon garlic powder
1 teaspoon cayenne
1¹/₂ teaspoons lemon pepper
¹/₂ cup water
1 pound shrimp

Combine butter, bay leaf, lemon juice, garlic powder, cayenne, lemon pepper and water in large pot. Heat until butter melts.

Arrange shrimp in single layer in shallow glass baking dish. Pour butter mixture over shrimp.

Bake at 350 degrees for 40 minutes. Remove bay leaf.

Serve immediately from baking dish. Serve with French bread for dipping in butter sauce.

Yield: 4 servings

Tandoori Shrimp

3¹/₂ pounds large shrimp
¹/₄ cup nonfat plain yogurt
4 large cloves of garlic, chopped
5 teaspoons fresh lemon juice
1¹/₂ teaspoons roasted cumin seeds
¹/₄ teaspoon garam masala
1 teaspoon cayenne
2 fresh hot green chiles, minced
Salt and pepper to taste

Peel shrimp; make cut in backs so shrimp can be flattened.

Combine yogurt, garlic, lemon juice, cumin seeds, garam masala, cayenne and green chiles in large bowl and mix well. Add shrimp. Marinate in refrigerator for 4 hours to overnight.

Remove shrimp from marinade. Season with salt and pepper. Thread on skewers.

Grill for 2 minutes per side.

Serve with basmati rice.

Garam masala is available at ethnic markets.

Yield: 4 to 6 servings

Herb Mayonnaise for Fish

1 cup mayonnaise
1 tablespoon minced fresh tarragon
1 tablespoon minced fresh basil
2 teaspoons freshly squeezed lemon juice
Salt and white pepper to taste

Combine mayonnaise, tarragon, basil, lemon juice, salt and white pepper in small bowl and blend well. Adjust seasonings.
Chill for 1 hour.
May also be used for poultry.

Yield: $^3/_4$ cup

Lemon Butter Patties

$^1/_2$ cup butter, softened
Juice and grated peel of $^1/_2$ lemon
1 tablespoon finely chopped scallions
$^1/_4$ teaspoon seasoned salt
$^1/_8$ teaspoon freshly ground pepper

Combine butter, lemon juice, lemon peel, scallions, seasoned salt and pepper in small bowl and mix well.
Shape into 1x7-inch roll on waxed paper. Chill until firm.
Slice and serve over fish.
May be melted and used as basting sauce.

Yield: $^1/_2$ cup

SEAFOOD

Green Peppercorn Butter

$^1/_2$ cup unsalted butter, softened
$^1/_4$ cup chopped fresh parsley
1 tablespoon green peppercorns, drained
1 teaspoon freshly squeezed lemon juice
$^1/_2$ teaspoon Dijon mustard
Worcestershire sauce to taste
Salt to taste (optional)

Combine butter, parsley, peppercorns, lemon juice, Dijon mustard, Worcestershire sauce and salt in food processor container. Process until well blended.

Chill until serving time.

Use with fish, omelets or grilled meat.

Yield: $^1/_2$ cup

Red Pepper Sauce

4 medium red bell peppers, chopped
1 small yellow onion, chopped
1 clove of garlic, crushed
$^1/_8$ teaspoon hot pepper flakes, or to taste
1 tablespoon walnut oil
1 tablespoon red wine vinegar
1 tablespoon freshly squeezed lemon juice

Combine red peppers, onion, garlic, hot pepper flakes, walnut oil, vinegar and lemon juice in saucepan. Simmer for 30 minutes. Let cool.

Pour into food processor container. Process until smooth. Strain through sieve.

Serve warm with prawns.

Yield: 1 cup

SEAFOOD

Hyde Park

Hyde Park, just south of the business loop and adjacent to the lakefront, is known for its many significant contributions that make Chicago the world-class city it is. This integrated, middle-class community on the south shore is home to one of the most prestigious universities in the country, the University of Chicago. The university was founded on the northern side of the Midway Plaisance between Washington Park and Jackson Park, which was the location of the World's Columbian Exposition of 1893. The Museum of Science and Industry is the only survivor of the fair's classical design.

The DuSable Museum of African-American History, named for Chicago's first settler, black Haitian trader Jean Baptiste Pointe duSable, is also located in this area, as is the architecturally significant Robie House. The Robie House was built by Frank Lloyd Wright as a private residence.

Today, Hyde Park is known for having a thriving academic environment, offbeat shops and some of the most beautiful single-family homes in the city.

The University of Chicago

Champagne & Dessert Buffet

Champagne Punch 33

Chocolate Cognac Truffle Tartlets 230

Poppy Seed Orange Cheesecake 226

Frango Mint Chocolate Cookies 217

Italian Cream Cake 209

Grand Marnier Brownies 221

DESSERTS

Chocolate Cognac Truffle Tartlets

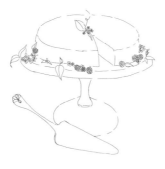

Desserts

Chocolate Cinnamon Cake

2 cups flour
2 cups sugar
1 cup butter
$^1/_4$ cup baking cocoa
1 cup water
$^1/_2$ cup buttermilk
1 teaspoon baking soda
1 teaspoon cinnamon
1 teaspoon vanilla extract

2 eggs
1 teaspoon salt
$^1/_2$ cup butter
$^1/_4$ cup baking cocoa
6 tablespoons milk
1 teaspoon vanilla extract
1 (1-pound) package
confectioners' sugar
1 cup pecan pieces

Sift flour and sugar into large bowl.

Bring 1 cup butter, $^1/_4$ cup cocoa and water to a boil in saucepan. Pour over flour mixture; mix well. Add buttermilk, baking soda, cinnamon, 1 teaspoon vanilla, eggs and salt and mix well. Pour into greased and floured 10x15-inch cake pan.

Bake at 400 degrees for 30 to 35 minutes or until wooden pick inserted near center comes out clean.

Bring $^1/_2$ cup butter, $^1/_4$ cup cocoa, milk and 1 teaspoon vanilla to a boil in saucepan; remove from heat. Add confectioners' sugar gradually, mixing until of spreading consistency. Stir in pecans. Spread over hot cake.

Cake may be baked in 9x13-inch cake pan for 40 to 50 minutes.

This is a great cake to make when you are short on time or want to make it ahead. It is always a hit.

Yield: 18 to 24 servings

DESSERTS

Carrot Cake with Cream Cheese Frosting

2 cups flour
2 teaspoons baking soda
2 teaspoons cinnamon
1 teaspoon salt
1 cup vegetable oil
1^3/$_4$ cups sugar
3 eggs
2 teaspoons vanilla extract
2 cups shredded carrots

1 cup flaked coconut
1 cup chopped pecans or walnuts
1 (8-ounce) can crushed pineapple
3 ounces cream cheese, softened
^{1}/$_2$ cup butter, softened
2 cups confectioners' sugar
1 teaspoon vanilla extract
^{1}/$_4$ to ^{1}/$_2$ cup chopped pecans or walnuts

Sift flour, baking soda, cinnamon and salt together.

Combine oil, sugar, eggs and 2 teaspoons vanilla in large bowl and mix well with wooden spoon. Stir in carrots, coconut, 1 cup pecans and undrained pineapple. Add flour mixture gradually, mixing well after each addition. Pour into 2 greased and floured cake pans.

Bake at 350 degrees for 40 minutes or until layers test done. Cool in pans for several minutes. Remove to wire rack to cool completely.

Beat cream cheese and butter in mixer bowl until smooth. Add confectioners' sugar and 1 teaspoon vanilla. Beat until of spreading consistency. Spread between layers and over top and side of cake. Sprinkle with ^{1}/$_4$ to ^{1}/$_2$ cup pecans.

Yield: 12 servings

DESSERTS

Italian Cream Cake

1 cup margarine or butter, softened
2 cups sugar
5 egg yolks
2 cups flour, sifted
1 teaspoon baking soda
1 cup buttermilk
1 teaspoon vanilla extract
1 (3-ounce) can flaked coconut
5 egg whites, stiffly beaten
8 ounces cream cheese, softened
1/4 cup margarine or butter, softened
1 (1-pound) package confectioners' sugar, sifted
1 teaspoon vanilla extract

Combine 1 cup margarine, sugar, egg yolks, flour, baking soda and buttermilk in large bowl and mix well. Stir in 1 teaspoon vanilla and coconut. Fold in egg whites. Pour into greased and floured 9x13-inch cake pan.

Bake at 350 degrees for 40 minutes. Cool in pan.

Beat cream cheese, 1/4 cup margarine, confectioners' sugar and 1 teaspoon vanilla in mixer bowl until of spreading consistency. Spread over cooled cake.

Yield: 15 servings

Coconut Pound Cake

6 egg yolks
1 cup shortening
1/2 cup unsalted butter, softened
3 cups sugar
1/2 teaspoon almond extract
1/2 teaspoon coconut extract
3 cups sifted cake flour
1 cup milk
2 cups grated canned or fresh coconut
6 egg whites, at room temperature

Cream egg yolks, shortening, butter and sugar at high speed in large mixing bowl until light and fluffy. Beat in flavorings. Add flour and milk alternately, beating at low speed after each addition and beginning and ending with flour. Add coconut and beat until well mixed.

Beat egg whites in medium mixing bowl until stiff peaks form. Fold into batter with wire whisk. Pour into greased and floured 10-inch tube pan.

Bake at 300 degrees for 2 hours. Cool in pan on wire rack for 45 minutes. Invert onto serving plate.

Yield: 12 to 15 servings

DESSERTS

Lemon Poppy Seed Cake

$^1/_3$ cup poppy seeds
1 cup plus 5 tablespoons sugar
2$^1/_2$ cups flour, sifted
1$^1/_2$ teaspoons baking powder
$^1/_2$ teaspoon baking soda
$^1/_8$ teaspoon salt
1$^1/_4$ teaspoons grated lemon peel
$^1/_3$ cup applesauce
1 cup evaporated skim milk

$^1/_4$ cup freshly squeezed lemon juice
2 teaspoons vanilla extract
3 egg whites
3 tablespoons sugar
1 package lemon pudding mix
3 tablespoons sugar
1$^1/_2$ tablespoons water
3 tablespoons lemon juice

Spray bundt pan with nonstick cooking spray; dust with flour.

Arrange poppy seeds on nonstick baking sheet. Bake at 350 degrees for 5 to 7 minutes or until toasted.

Combine 1 cup plus 5 tablespoons sugar, flour, baking powder, baking soda, salt and lemon peel in large bowl. Make a well in center.

Whisk applesauce, skim milk, $^1/_4$ cup lemon juice and vanilla in small bowl until creamy; set aside.

Beat egg whites in mixer bowl until foamy. Add 3 tablespoons sugar gradually, beating constantly until soft peaks form.

Add applesauce mixture to well in flour mixture and stir gently. Fold in egg whites, poppy seeds and pudding mix. Spoon into prepared pan.

Bake at 350 degrees in lower third of oven for 50 minutes or until wooden pick inserted near center comes out clean.

Cool in pan for 30 minutes. Invert onto cake plate.

Combine 3 tablespoons sugar and water in small saucepan. Cook over medium heat for 2 to 3 minutes or until syrupy. Stir in 3 tablespoons lemon juice.

Pierce top and side of cake several times. Drizzle syrup over cake by spoonfuls, allowing cake to absorb syrup between spoonfuls.

Cool for 1 hour.

Yield: 16 servings

DESSERTS

Baumkuchen
(Vanilla and Chocolate Layered Cake)

¹/₃ cup semisweet chocolate chips
¹/₂ cup butter, softened
¹/₂ cup sugar
1 teaspoon vanilla extract
7 egg yolks
²/₃ cup flour
3 tablespoons cornstarch
7 egg whites
¹/₄ cup sugar

²/₃ cup sour cream
3 tablespoons sugar
¹/₂ teaspoon lemon juice
²/₃ cup semisweet chocolate chips
3 tablespoons butter
¹/₃ cup sour cream
¹/₄ teaspoon vanilla extract
2 to 2¹/₂ cups confectioners' sugar
Fresh strawberries

Melt ¹/₃ cup chocolate chips in double boiler over simmering water.

Beat ¹/₂ cup butter, ¹/₂ cup sugar and 1 teaspoon vanilla in mixer bowl until fluffy. Beat in egg yolks 1 at a time. Stir in mixture of flour and cornstarch. Divide batter between 2 bowls. Stir melted chocolate into 1 bowl.

Beat egg whites in mixing bowl until soft peaks form. Add ¹/₄ cup sugar gradually, beating constantly until stiff peaks form. Fold half the beaten egg whites into each batter.

Spread ¹/₂ cup chocolate batter in greased 9-inch springform pan. Place pan under preheated broiler 5 inches from heat source. Broil for 1 to 2 minutes or until baked.

Spread ¹/₂ cup plain batter over chocolate layer. Broil for 1 to 2 minutes or until baked. Repeat process until all batter is used.

Blend ²/₃ cup sour cream, 3 tablespoons sugar and lemon juice in bowl. Spread over top of cake. Broil for 1 minute. Cool for 15 minutes. Remove sides of pan and cool completely.

Melt ²/₃ cup chocolate chips and 3 tablespoons butter in double boiler over simmering water, stirring until smooth. Pour into small bowl. Cool for 10 minutes. Stir in ¹/₃ cup sour cream and vanilla. Add confectioners' sugar gradually, beating until smooth and of spreading consistency. Spread ²/₃ of the frosting over side of cake. Pipe remaining frosting onto top of cake in decorative design. Top with fresh strawberries.

Yield: 12 servings

DESSERTS

Almond Crunch Cookies

1 cup sugar
1 cup confectioners' sugar
1 cup butter, softened
1 cup vegetable oil
1 teaspoon almond extract
2 eggs
3^1/$_2$ cups all-purpose flour

1 cup whole wheat flour
1 teaspoon baking soda
1 teaspoon salt
1 teaspoon cream of tartar
2 cups chopped almonds
7^1/$_2$ ounces brickle chips

Combine sugar, confectioners' sugar, butter and oil in large bowl and mix well. Stir in flavoring and eggs. Add flour, baking soda, salt and cream of tartar and blend well. Stir in almonds and brickle chips. May chill dough at this point.

Shape by tablespoonfuls into balls. Roll in additional sugar. Place on nonstick cookie sheets. Flatten in crisscross pattern with fork dipped in additional sugar.

Bake at 350 degrees for 12 to 18 minutes or until edges are golden brown. Cool on cookie sheets for 1 minute. Remove to wire rack to cool completely.

Yield: 3^1/$_2$ dozen

DESSERTS

Sugar Cookies

2$^{1}/_{2}$ cups flour, sifted
2 teaspoons baking powder
$^{1}/_{2}$ teaspoon salt
1$^{1}/_{2}$ cups confectioners' sugar
1 egg
1 cup butter, softened
1 teaspoon vanilla extract
Tinted decorator sugar

Sift flour, baking powder, salt and confectioners' sugar into large bowl.

Blend egg, butter and vanilla in medium bowl. Add to flour mixture and mix until dough forms a ball. Chill, wrapped in waxed paper, for 2 hours.

Divide dough into 3 portions. Roll each portion $^{3}/_{16}$ inch thick on floured surface. Cut with favorite cookie cutter. Place on nonstick cookie sheet. Sprinkle with decorator sugar.

Bake at 350 degrees for 8 minutes.

Yield: 2$^{1}/_{2}$ dozen

Caramel Grahams

10 to 12 graham crackers
$^{1}/_{2}$ cup butter
$^{1}/_{2}$ cup margarine
1 cup packed brown sugar
1 cup chopped pecans or walnuts

Arrange graham crackers in single layer on greased cookie sheet with sides.

Melt butter and margarine in medium saucepan. Add brown sugar. Boil for 2 minutes. Spread evenly over graham crackers. Sprinkle with pecans.

Bake at 350 degrees for 15 minutes. Let cool. Break into pieces.

Yield: 2 to 2$^{1}/_{2}$ dozen

Peanut Butter Oatmeal Cookies

1 cup flour
$^1/_2$ teaspoon baking soda
$^1/_2$ cup corn syrup
$^1/_2$ cup natural peanut butter
2 egg whites
$^1/_3$ cup sugar
$^1/_3$ cup packed brown sugar
$^1/_2$ teaspoon vanilla extract
1 cup rolled oats

Mix flour and baking soda together.

Combine corn syrup and peanut butter in large bowl and mix well. Add egg whites, sugar, brown sugar and vanilla. Add flour mixture and mix well. Fold in oats.

Drop by rounded teaspoonfuls onto nonstick cookie sheet.

Bake at 375 degrees for 8 minutes.

Yield: 2 dozen

German Brownie Drops

2 bars German's sweet chocolate
1 tablespoon butter
2 eggs
$^3/_4$ cup sugar
$^1/_4$ cup flour
$^1/_4$ teaspoon baking powder
$^1/_4$ teaspoon cinnamon
$^1/_8$ teaspoon salt
$^1/_2$ teaspoon vanilla extract
$^1/_4$ cup finely chopped pecans
$^1/_4$ cup finely chopped walnuts

Melt chocolate and butter in double boiler over hot water, stirring until smooth. Let cool.

Beat eggs in mixing bowl until foamy. Add sugar 2 tablespoons at a time, beating well after each addition. Beat for 5 minutes or until thickened.

Blend in chocolate. Add flour, baking powder, cinnamon and salt and blend well. Stir in vanilla, pecans and walnuts. Let stand for 5 to 10 minutes or until firm.

Drop by teaspoonfuls onto nonstick cookie sheet.

Bake at 350 degrees for 8 to 10 minutes or until cookies feel set when lightly touched. Cool on cookie sheet for 5 minutes. Remove to wire rack to cool completely.

Yield: 3 dozen

DESSERTS

Pine Nut Brown Sugar Shortbread

$^1/_2$ cup unsalted butter, softened
$^1/_3$ cup confectioners' sugar
3 tablespoons light brown sugar
$^1/_2$ teaspoon vanilla extract
1 cup plus 1 tablespoon flour
$^1/_2$ teaspoon cinnamon
$^1/_4$ teaspoon salt
$^1/_3$ cup pine nuts

Cream butter, confectioners' sugar and brown sugar in mixing bowl until light and fluffy. Beat in vanilla. Add flour, cinnamon and salt, mixing until crumbly. Press evenly into 9-inch fluted tart pan with removable bottom. Score edge lightly with fork tines. Press pine nuts over center of dough.

Bake at 325 degrees for 35 minutes or until browned and fairly firm. Cool in pan for 15 minutes. Score into 12 to 16 wedges. Cool completely in pan. Dust with additional confectioners' sugar.

Yield: 12 to 16 servings

Victorian Tea Hearts

1 cup butter, softened
$1^1/_2$ cups flour
1 cup sugar
$^1/_4$ teaspoon salt
4 eggs
1 tablespoon amaretto
$^1/_2$ to $^3/_4$ cup apricot or peach preserves
Sifted confectioners' sugar
Sweetened whipped cream
Mandarin orange slices

Beat butter in food processor until creamy. Add mixture of flour, sugar and salt. Process for 5 minutes.

Add eggs and liqueur. Process for 5 minutes. Spoon into greased jelly roll pan.

Bake at 350 degrees for 18 minutes or until wooden pick inserted near center comes out clean. Cool in pan for 10 minutes. Cut with 2-inch heart-shaped cookie cutter.

Spread 1 teaspoon preserves over each heart. Top with another heart. Dust with confectioners' sugar. Top with swirl of whipped cream and mandarin orange slice.

Yield: $2^1/_2$ dozen

DESSERTS

Koulourakia

1 cup butter, softened
$^1/_2$ cup sugar
1 egg
1 egg white
3 cups sifted flour
1 teaspoon baking powder
1 tablespoon lemon juice or orange juice
1 egg yolk
2 tablespoons water
Sesame seeds

Beat butter in mixing bowl until creamy. Add sugar gradually, beating well after each addition.

Add egg and 1 egg white and beat well. Stir in flour and baking powder. Blend in lemon juice.

Knead until smooth dough forms. Pinch off tablespoon-size pieces. Roll each piece 6 inches long on lightly floured board. Bend each piece in center and twist 2 sides together into ropes. Place on nonstick cookie sheet.

Mix 1 egg yolk and water in bowl. Brush over each rope. Sprinkle with sesame seeds.

Bake at 350 degrees for 15 minutes or until lightly browned.

Serve with coffee or tea.

Yield: 24 to 30 servings

Orange and Cinnamon Biscotti

2 cups flour
$1^1/_2$ teaspoons baking powder
1 teaspoon ground cinnamon
$^1/_4$ teaspoon salt
1 cup sugar
$^1/_2$ cup unsalted butter, softened
2 eggs
1 tablespoon grated orange peel
1 teaspoon vanilla extract

Mix flour, baking powder, cinnamon and salt in large bowl. Make well in center.

Beat sugar and butter in mixing bowl until blended. Beat in eggs 1 at a time. Beat in orange peel and vanilla. Add to well in flour mixture, stirring just until mixed.

Divide dough into 2 equal portions. Shape each portion into a $1x2^1/_2$-inch log. Place on cookie sheet sprayed with nonstick cooking spray.

Bake at 325 degrees for 35 minutes or until firm. Cool on cookie sheet for 10 minutes. Remove to work surface.

Cut diagonally into $^1/_2$-inch slices with serrated knife. Arrange cut side down on cookie sheet sprayed with nonstick cooking spray.

Bake at 325 degrees for 24 minutes or until golden brown on both sides, turning once.

Yield: $1^1/_2$ to 2 dozen

Cappuccino Flats

2 cups flour
1 teaspoon cinnamon
$^1/_4$ teaspoon salt
1 cup butter, softened
$^1/_2$ cup packed brown sugar
$^1/_2$ cup sugar
2 ounces unsweetened chocolate, melted
1 tablespoon instant espresso coffee
1 egg
1 cup semisweet chocolate chips
2 tablespoons butter

Mix flour, cinnamon and salt together.

Cream 1 cup butter, brown sugar and sugar in mixing bowl until light and fluffy. Stir in melted chocolate, coffee and egg. Add flour mixture and mix well.

Divide dough into 4 equal portions. Chill for 1 hour.

Roll into four 6-inch rolls on waxed paper. Freeze for 30 minutes.

Cut rolls into $^1/_4$-inch slices. Place on greased cookie sheet.

Bake at 350 degrees for 10 to 12 minutes or until lightly browned. Remove to wire rack to cool.

Melt chocolate chips and 2 tablespoons butter in double boiler over simmering water. Dip half of each cookie into chocolate mixture. Let stand on waxed paper until set.

Yield: 1$^1/_2$ to 2 dozen

Frango Mint Chocolate Cookies

This recipe was contributed by Marshall Field's.

1 cup unsalted butter, softened
$^1/_2$ cup confectioners' sugar
2 cups cake flour
1 teaspoon vanilla extract
$^1/_8$ teaspoon salt
1 cup finely chopped pecans
18 Frango mint chocolates,
cut into halves vertically
Confectioners' sugar

Combine butter and $^1/_2$ cup confectioners' sugar in medium bowl. Beat with handheld mixer at medium speed for 1 minute. Add flour, vanilla and salt, mixing well with wooden spoon. Stir in pecans. Chill, loosely covered with plastic wrap, for 1 hour or until dough is firm enough to handle.

Enclose each mint half in approximately 1 tablespoon dough. Shape each into a ball. Place 1 inch apart on 2 nonstick cookie sheets. Place 1 cookie sheet on center rack of oven and 1 on top rack.

Bake at 350 degrees for 10 minutes. Switch position of cookie sheets. Bake for 8 to 10 minutes longer or until golden brown.

Sift additional confectioners' sugar into a medium bowl. Roll cookies in confectioners' sugar until well coated. Cool on wire rack.

Yield: 3 dozen

Pepperkaker
(Swedish Spice Cookies)

5 cups flour, sifted
1 teaspoon baking powder
1 teaspoon baking soda
1 teaspoon cloves
1¹/₂ teaspoons cinnamon
1 cup sugar
1 cup butter, softened
1 egg
1 cup dark molasses

Sift flour, baking powder, baking soda, cloves and cinnamon together.

Cream sugar and butter in mixing bowl until light and fluffy. Beat in egg and molasses. Add flour mixture gradually, beating well after each addition.

Chill for 1 to 2 days. Roll very thin on lightly floured surface. Cut into assorted shapes with cookie cutters. Place on nonstick cookie sheet.

Bake at 300 degrees for 8 minutes or until lightly browned.

May shape chilled dough into log and slice very thin instead of rolling and cutting with cookie cutters.

Yield: 8 to 10 dozen

Best Gingerbread
Cookies

5 cups sifted flour
1¹/₂ teaspoons baking soda
¹/₂ teaspoon salt
2 teaspoons cinnamon
1 teaspoon ginger
1 teaspoon cloves
1 cup shortening
1 cup sugar
1 egg
1 cup molasses
1 tablespoon vinegar

Sift flour, baking soda, salt, cinnamon, ginger and cloves together.

Cream shortening and sugar in mixer bowl until light and fluffy. Add egg, molasses and vinegar and beat well. Add flour mixture and mix well.

Chill for 3 hours. Roll on lightly floured surface. Cut with cookie cutter. Place on nonstick cookie sheet.

Bake at 375 degrees for 5 to 6 minutes or until browned.

Yield: 8 to 10 dozen

Frank Lloyd Wright's Prairie-style Robie House

Elephant Cookies

2 cups flour
2 teaspoons baking soda
1 teaspoon baking powder
1 teaspoon salt
2 cups shortening
2 cups sugar
1^1/$_3$ cups packed brown sugar
4 eggs
2 teaspoons vanilla extract
4 cups rolled oats
4 cups cornflakes
1 cup chocolate chips
1 cup raisins (optional)

Sift flour, baking soda, baking powder and salt together.

Cream shortening, sugar and brown sugar in large mixing bowl until light and fluffy. Beat in eggs 1 at a time. Add flour mixture gradually, beating well after each addition. Stir in vanilla.

Add oats 1 cup at a time, beating well after each addition. Add cornflakes 1 cup at a time. Stir in chocolate chips and raisins.

Drop by ice cream scoopful 2 inches apart onto nonstick cookie sheet.

Bake at 350 degrees for 10 to 15 minutes or until lightly browned. Cool on cookie sheet for several minutes. Remove to waxed paper to cool completely.

Yield: 3 dozen

Apricot Bars

^{2}/$_3$ cup dried apricots
^{1}/$_2$ cup butter
^{1}/$_4$ cup sugar
1^1/$_3$ cups flour
^{1}/$_2$ teaspoon baking powder
^{1}/$_4$ teaspoon salt
2 eggs
1 cup packed brown sugar
^{1}/$_2$ teaspoon vanilla extract
^{1}/$_2$ cup chopped walnuts
Confectioners' sugar

Rinse apricots. Combine with water to cover in saucepan. Boil for 10 minutes. Drain and let cool. Chop into pieces.

Mix butter, sugar and 1 cup of the flour in bowl until crumbly. Press into greased 8x8-inch baking pan. Bake at 350 degrees for 25 minutes or until lightly browned.

Sift remaining ^{1}/$_3$ cup flour, baking powder and salt together.

Beat eggs in mixing bowl. Add brown sugar gradually, beating well after each addition. Add flour mixture and mix well. Stir in vanilla, walnuts and apricots. Spread over baked crust.

Bake at 350 degrees for 30 minutes or until set. Cool in pan. Cut into bars. Roll in confectioners' sugar.

Yield: 32 servings

Grand Marnier Brownies

6 ounces bittersweet chocolate
$^3/_4$ cup butter
4 eggs
$1^1/_2$ cups sugar
$^1/_2$ cup whipping cream
1 tablespoon Grand Marnier
2 teaspoons grated orange peel
$^1/_2$ teaspoon orange oil
$^1/_4$ teaspoon vanilla extract
$^3/_4$ cup flour
$^1/_4$ teaspoon salt

Melt chocolate and butter in double boiler over hot water or in heavy saucepan over low heat. Let cool.

Beat eggs and sugar in mixing bowl until thick and pale yellow. Beat in whipping cream, Grand Marnier, orange peel, orange oil and vanilla. Beat in chocolate mixture. Add flour and salt and mix well. Spread evenly in buttered and floured 9x13-inch baking pan.

Bake at 350 degrees for 25 minutes or until edges pull away from pan and/or wooden pick inserted near center comes out clean. Let cool. Cut into squares.

Yield: 4 dozen

Raspberry Brownies

1 cup unsalted butter, softened
$1^1/_4$ cups sugar
$^1/_2$ cup packed brown sugar
4 eggs
$^1/_2$ cup baking cocoa
1 tablespoon framboise (raspberry brandy)
1 teaspoon vanilla extract
$^1/_4$ teaspoon salt
$1^1/_4$ cups flour
$1^1/_2$ pints fresh raspberries
4 ounces semisweet chocolate, chopped
2 tablespoons framboise
2 teaspoons hot water
Confectioners' sugar (optional)

Cream butter, sugar and brown sugar in large mixer bowl until light and fluffy. Beat in eggs 1 at a time. Stir in cocoa, 1 tablespoon framboise, vanilla and salt. Add flour and mix gently. Pour into greased 9x13-inch baking pan. Sprinkle evenly with raspberries.

Bake at 325 degrees for 30 minutes or until wooden pick inserted near center comes out clean. Cool in pan on wire rack. Cut into 2x3-inch bars.

Heat chocolate, 2 tablespoons framboise and hot water in double boiler over barely simmering water, stirring until smooth. Cool slightly.

Sift confectioners' sugar over brownies. Dip brownies in glaze and/or drizzle glaze decoratively over brownies. Let stand until glaze is set.

Yield: 16 servings

DESSERTS

White Chocolate Brownies

2 cups flour
2 teaspoons baking powder
$^1/_2$ teaspoon salt
1 (1-pound) package dark
brown sugar
$^3/_4$ cup unsalted butter
3 tablespoons instant coffee
1 tablespoon hot water

2 eggs
2 tablespoons Kahlúa
1 cup chopped white chocolate
$^1/_2$ cup chopped pecans or walnuts
$^1/_3$ cup caramel-butterscotch sauce
5 tablespoons water
1 teaspoon crème de cacao
1 teaspoon Kahlúa

Sift flour, baking powder and salt together.

Heat brown sugar and butter in saucepan until butter melts, stirring frequently. Dissolve coffee powder in 1 tablespoon hot water. Stir into brown sugar mixture. Cool to room temperature.

Whisk in eggs and 2 tablespoons Kahlúa. Add flour mixture and mix well. Stir in white chocolate and pecans. Spread in buttered 10-inch cake pan.

Bake at 350 degrees for 35 to 40 minutes or until golden brown.

Bring caramel-butterscotch sauce, 5 tablespoons water, crème de cacao and 1 teaspoon Kahlúa to a boil in saucepan.

Prick brownies with fork. Drizzle with caramel mixture.

Yield: 12 to 15 servings

DESSERTS

Apple Torte with Butterscotch Sauce

1 egg
1 cup sugar
$^1/_4$ cup butter, softened
1 cup flour
1 teaspoon baking soda
$^1/_2$ teaspoon nutmeg
$^1/_2$ teaspoon cinnamon
$^1/_2$ teaspoon salt
2 cups chopped apples
$^1/_4$ to $^1/_2$ cup chopped walnuts
$^1/_2$ cup butter
$^1/_2$ cup packed brown sugar
$^1/_2$ cup sugar
$^1/_2$ cup cream

Beat egg, 1 cup sugar and $^1/_4$ cup butter in mixing bowl. Add flour, baking soda, nutmeg, cinnamon and salt and mix well. Stir in apples. Pour into greased 8x8-inch baking pan. Sprinkle with walnuts.

Bake at 350 degrees for 30 to 40 minutes or until wooden pick inserted near center comes out clean. Cool in pan.

Bring $^1/_2$ cup butter, brown sugar, $^1/_2$ cup sugar and cream to a boil in saucepan. Drizzle over torte.

Yield: 8 servings

Blueberry Cobbler

3 cups fresh blueberries or other fresh fruit
$^1/_4$ cup packed brown sugar
1 tablespoon cornstarch
$^1/_8$ teaspoon nutmeg
1 tablespoon butter
1 cup sifted flour
$^1/_2$ cup sugar
$1^1/_2$ teaspoons baking powder
$^1/_2$ teaspoon salt
$^1/_8$ teaspoon nutmeg
$^1/_2$ cup milk
$^1/_4$ cup melted butter
1 to 2 teaspoons sugar

Combine blueberries, brown sugar, cornstarch and $^1/_8$ teaspoon nutmeg in saucepan. Cook until thickened, stirring frequently. Stir in 1 tablespoon butter.

Sift flour, $^1/_2$ cup sugar, baking powder, salt and $^1/_8$ teaspoon nutmeg into bowl. Add milk and melted butter all at once and mix well.

Pour hot blueberry mixture into baking dish. Pour milk mixture over blueberries. Sprinkle with 1 to 2 teaspoons sugar.

Bake at 350 degrees for 30 minutes or until lightly browned.

Serve with cream or ice cream.

Yield: 6 to 8 servings

DESSERTS

Plum Pudding

1 pound raisins
1 pound currants
8 ounces mixed orange, citron and lemon peel
1 cup flour
1 cup sugar
1 cup bread crumbs
1 pound suet
$2^1/_4$ teaspoons cinnamon
$2^1/_4$ teaspoons cloves
1 teaspoon nutmeg
1 teaspoon mace
6 eggs
$^1/_8$ teaspoon baking soda
2 teaspoons hot water

Combine raisins, currants, mixed peel and flour in large bowl, stirring until fruit is coated.

Stir in sugar, bread crumbs and suet. Add cinnamon, cloves, nutmeg and mace.

Add eggs and mixture of baking soda and hot water and mix well. Pour into greased pudding mold. Steam for 3 hours.

Serve with Heavenly Hard Sauce (page 233).

Yield: 10 servings

Tiramisù

6 egg yolks
$1^1/_4$ cups sugar
$1^1/_4$ cups mascarpone cheese
$1^3/_4$ cups whipping cream, whipped
2 (3-ounce) packages ladyfingers,
split into halves
$^1/_3$ cup Kahlúa
Sweetened whipped cream
Chocolate curls

Beat egg yolks and sugar in mixing bowl until thick and pale yellow. Pour into double boiler over boiling water; reduce heat to low. Cook for 8 to 10 minutes or until thickened, stirring constantly. Remove from heat.

Add cheese and beat well. Fold in whipped cream.

Line bottom and side of $2^1/_2$-quart bowl or trifle dish with half the ladyfingers, split side up. Brush with half the Kahlúa. Top with half the egg yolk mixture. Repeat layers.

Top with sweetened whipped cream and chocolate curls.

Note: To prepare sweetened whipped cream, beat $^1/_2$ cup whipping cream, 1 tablespoon confectioners' sugar and $^1/_4$ teaspoon vanilla in small mixer bowl until stiff peaks form.

Yield: 8 to 10 servings

DESSERTS

Chocolate Soufflés with Chocolate Sauce

8 ounces semisweet chocolate
9 tablespoons unsalted butter
2 tablespoons baking cocoa
4 egg yolks
4 egg whites
6 tablespoons sugar
4 ounces semisweet chocolate
$^1/_3$ cup baking cocoa
1 cup water
$^1/_2$ cup sugar
$^1/_2$ cup corn syrup

Melt 8 ounces chocolate, butter and 2 tablespoons cocoa in saucepan. Remove from heat. Stir a small amount of hot mixture into egg yolks; stir egg yolks into hot mixture.

Beat egg whites with 6 tablespoons sugar in mixing bowl. Fold into chocolate mixture.

Fill buttered and sugared small ramekins $^3/_4$ full with chocolate mixture. Bake at 400 degrees for 5 to 6 minutes or until puffed.

Combine 4 ounces chocolate, $^1/_3$ cup cocoa, water, $^1/_2$ cup sugar and corn syrup in metal bowl or double boiler. Cook over steam until chocolate is melted, stirring until smooth. Strain through a sieve. Serve warm or cool over soufflés.

May prepare soufflés ahead. Cover and store in refrigerator for up to 2 days.

Yield: 4 to 6 servings

Chocolate Bread Pudding with Sauce

1 cup raisins
$^1/_2$ cup coffee liqueur
1 (1-pound) loaf dried French bread
2 cups milk
2 cups half-and-half
5 eggs
$1^1/_2$ cups sugar
3 tablespoons baking cocoa
1 tablespoon cinnamon
2 cups semisweet chocolate chips
$^1/_4$ cup butter
$^3/_4$ cup confectioners' sugar
1 cup coffee liqueur

Boil raisins in $^1/_2$ cup liqueur in saucepan for 5 minutes.

Tear bread into small pieces. Soak in mixture of milk and half-and-half in large bowl.

Add eggs, sugar, cocoa, cinnamon, chocolate chips and raisin mixture and mix lightly. Pour into greased 4-quart casserole.

Bake at 325 degrees for 1 hour. Let stand for 15 minutes.

Melt butter in saucepan. Add confectioners' sugar, stirring until smooth. Add 1 cup liqueur gradually, stirring after each addition. Cook for 2 minutes or until heated through, stirring until smooth. Serve over bread pudding.

Yield: 8 to 10 servings

DESSERTS

Poppy Seed Orange Cheesecake

1 cup blanched almonds
6 whole graham crackers
1 tablespoon sugar
6 tablespoons melted
unsalted butter
24 ounces cream cheese, softened
1 cup sugar
$^1/_2$ cup unsalted butter, softened
$1^1/_2$ tablespoons (or more)
grated orange peel

$^1/_2$ cup sour cream
$3^1/_2$ tablespoons orange juice
1 tablespoon vanilla extract
4 eggs
2 tablespoons poppy seeds
$1^1/_2$ cups sour cream
2 tablespoons orange juice
$1^1/_2$ tablespoons sugar

Grind almonds, graham crackers and 1 tablespoon sugar in food processor or blender. Add 6 tablespoons butter. Process until crumbs are evenly moistened. Press onto bottom and 1 inch up side of 10-inch springform pan.

Bake at 350 degrees for 8 minutes or until puffed. Cool in pan on wire rack.

Beat cream cheese, 1 cup sugar, $^1/_2$ cup butter and orange peel in large mixing bowl. Add $^1/_2$ cup sour cream, $3^1/_2$ tablespoons orange juice and vanilla, beating just until blended. Beat in eggs 1 at a time. Stir in poppy seeds. Pour into crust.

Bake at 350 degrees for 20 minutes. Decrease oven temperature to 300 degrees. Bake for 20 minutes. Decrease oven temperature to 250 degrees. Bake for 55 minutes or until center is barely set.

Blend $1^1/_2$ cups sour cream, 2 tablespoons orange juice and $1^1/_2$ tablespoons sugar in bowl. Spoon over hot cheesecake.

Increase oven temperature to 350 degrees. Bake for 8 minutes or until topping is set. Cool in pan on wire rack.

Run small knife around top edge of cake to loosen topping from side. Chill, covered, for 8 to 10 hours.

Run small knife around edge of cake to loosen from pan. Serve alone or with raspberry purée sauce.

Yield: 10 servings

DESSERTS

Peach Shortcake

2 cups flour
1 tablespoon baking powder
$^1/_4$ cup sugar
1 teaspoon salt
$^1/_4$ teaspoon nutmeg
$^1/_2$ cup frozen butter
$^1/_2$ cup mashed roasted sweet potato
$^3/_4$ cup whipping cream
$^1/_2$ cup packed brown sugar

2 cups sugar
$^1/_8$ teaspoon salt
1 cup water
1 tablespoon lemon juice
1 tablespoon orange juice
12 peaches, peeled, sliced
Sprigs of fresh mint
Whipped cream

Combine flour, baking powder, $^1/_4$ cup sugar, 1 teaspoon salt and nutmeg in mixing bowl. Add butter. Beat at low speed until crumbly.

Add sweet potato and mix until combined. Beat in enough of the whipping cream to form a soft dough.

Roll 1 inch thick on floured surface. Cut into circles with glass or cookie cutter. Place on parchment-lined baking sheet. Brush with remaining whipping cream. Sprinkle with brown sugar.

Bake at 350 degrees until golden brown.

Bring 2 cups sugar, $^1/_8$ teaspoon salt, water, lemon juice and orange juice to a boil in heavy saucepan. Cook until syrup begins to brown around edges. Add peaches; remove from heat. Let cool.

Spread peach syrup over top of each biscuit. Top with mint sprig and whipped cream.

Yield: $1^1/_2$ to 2 dozen

DESSERTS

Profiteroles

¹/₂ cup butter or margarine
1 cup hot water
1 cup flour
¹/₂ teaspoon salt
4 eggs

Ice cream, whipped cream
or pudding
Sliced fruit or chocolate sauce
(optional)

Bring butter and water to a boil in saucepan. Add flour and salt all at once. Cook over medium heat, stirring constantly until mixture leaves side of pan and forms stiff ball. Remove from heat.

Blend in eggs 1 at a time, beating well after each addition. Drop into 12 mounds 3 to 4 inches apart on nonstick baking sheet.

Bake at 425 degrees for 30 to 35 minutes or until golden brown. Turn off oven. Prick puffs with sharp knife to allow steam to escape. Let stand in oven for 20 minutes to dry centers.

Split puffs into halves horizontally. Fill with ice cream. Top with fruit. Replace tops.

May cover and store dough in refrigerator for up to 3 days. May drop dough into 36 small mounds for bite-size puffs. Baked profiteroles may be frozen, thawed and heated in 350-degree oven for 10 to 15 minutes or until crisp.

Yield: 12 servings

DESSERTS

Margarita Ice Cream Torte

30 chocolate sandwich cookies
$^1/_4$ cup melted butter or margarine
$^1/_2$ cup thawed frozen
lemonade concentrate
6 tablespoons Tequila
Grated peel of 1 lime

2 tablespoons plus 2 teaspoons
fresh lime juice
2 tablespoons Triple Sec
5 to 6 drops of green food coloring
2 quarts vanilla ice cream, softened

Process cookies in food processor until crumbly. Add butter. Process until combined. Reserve 2 tablespoons crumb mixture for garnish. Press remaining crumb mixture into oiled $8^1/_2$- or 9-inch springform pan. Bake at 350 degrees for 10 minutes. Let stand until cool.

Combine lemonade concentrate, Tequila, lime peel, lime juice, Triple Sec and food coloring in large bowl. Stir in ice cream until blended; do not let ice cream melt.

Spoon into cooled crust. Sprinkle reserved crumbs around top edge. Freeze, covered with foil, for 8 to 10 hours or until firm.

Remove side of springform pan. Remove torte to serving platter. Cut into wedges to serve.

Yield: 10 to 12 servings

DESSERTS

Chocolate Cognac Truffle Tartlets

1 cup flour
6 tablespoons baking cocoa
$^1/_8$ teaspoon salt, or to taste
$^1/_2$ cup unsalted butter, softened
$^1/_2$ cup packed light brown sugar
$1^1/_2$ teaspoons vanilla extract

$1^1/_4$ cups whipping cream
2 tablespoons unsalted butter
10 ounces bittersweet or semisweet
chocolate, chopped
3 tablespoons Cognac or brandy

Mix flour, cocoa and salt together.

Cream $^1/_2$ cup butter, brown sugar and vanilla in medium mixing bowl until light and fluffy. Add flour mixture, stirring with fork until crumbly. Gather dough into ball; flatten into disk. Chill, wrapped in plastic wrap, for 20 minutes or until dough begins to firm.

Divide dough into 4 equal portions. Press 1 portion evenly over bottom and up sides of each of four $4^1/_2$-inch tartlet pans with removable bottoms. Freeze for 20 minutes.

Line tartlet shells with foil; fill with dried beans or pie weights. Bake at 350 degrees for 20 minutes or until set. Remove beans and foil. Bake for 5 minutes longer or until crusts feel dry. Cool on wire rack.

Combine whipping cream and 2 tablespoons butter in medium saucepan. Cook over low heat until butter melts, stirring constantly. Add chocolate. Cook until melted, stirring constantly. Whisk in Cognac. Cool for 15 minutes.

Spoon $^1/_2$ cup filling into each crust. Cover tartlets and chill overnight.

Let tartlets stand at room temperature for 15 minutes. Cut some paper into $4^1/_2$x5-inch long strips. Arrange in lattice fashion over each tartlet. Sift additional cocoa over lattices; remove paper. Garnish with fresh raspberries, whipped cream and sprig of mint.

Start this recipe the day before serving the tartlets.

Yield: 4 to 8 servings

DESSERTS

Cranberry Crumb Tart

$^1/_2$ cup cold butter, cut into
$^1/_2$-inch pieces
1 cup plus 2 tablespoons flour
$1^1/_2$ teaspoons sugar
$^1/_8$ teaspoon salt
$^1/_4$ cup ice water
$1^1/_4$ cups flour

$1^3/_4$ cups sugar
$^3/_4$ cup cold butter, cut into
1-inch cubes
$^3/_4$ cup sugar
$^1/_2$ teaspoon salt
6 cups fresh cranberries

Cut $^1/_2$ cup butter into 1 cup plus 2 tablespoons flour in medium bowl until crumbly.

Dissolve $1^1/_2$ teaspoons sugar and $^1/_8$ teaspoon salt in ice water in small bowl. Sprinkle over flour mixture, tossing until soft dough forms.

Shape into ball on floured surface. Wrap in plastic wrap and flatten into 6-inch disk. Chill for 30 minutes or longer.

Roll into thin circle on lightly floured surface. Trim to 15-inch circle. Dust lightly with flour and fold into quarters. Place with point in center in 9- or 10-inch tart pan with removable bottom. Unfold and fit into pan, folding down excess to reinforce sides. Press against fluted sides of pan and trim excess. Chill, covered with plastic wrap, for 1 hour to overnight. Line pastry with foil; fill with pie weights or dried beans.

Bake at 425 degrees for 20 to 25 minutes or until almost dry. Remove weights and foil. Prick bottom and sides of crust with fork. Bake for 5 to 8 minutes longer or until golden brown.

Combine $1^1/_4$ cups flour and $1^3/_4$ cups sugar in large bowl. Cut in $^3/_4$ cup butter until crumbly.

Mix $^3/_4$ cup sugar with $^1/_2$ teaspoon salt in medium bowl. Add cranberries, tossing to coat.

Spoon cranberries into prepared tart pan, mounding slightly in center. Sprinkle flour mixture gently over cranberries; do not press topping into fruit.

Bake at 375 degrees for 40 minutes or until topping is golden brown and fruit is bubbling around edge. Serve at room temperature.

Yield: 8 servings

DESSERTS

Lemon Macaroon Pie

1 cup all-purpose flour
$^1/_3$ cup cake flour
1 tablespoon sugar
$^1/_2$ teaspoon salt
6 tablespoons chilled unsalted
butter, cut into 4 pieces
2 tablespoons chilled shortening,
cut into pieces
3 tablespoons (or more) ice water
3 eggs
2 egg yolks
$^1/_4$ teaspoon salt
$1^1/_4$ cups sugar

$1^1/_4$ cups sweetened
shredded coconut
$^1/_4$ cup chilled whipping cream
$^1/_4$ cup fresh lemon juice
2 tablespoons melted
unsalted butter
2 teaspoons grated lemon peel
$1^1/_2$ teaspoons vanilla extract
$^1/_2$ teaspoon almond extract
$^3/_4$ cup chilled whipping cream
2 teaspoons confectioners' sugar
$^3/_4$ teaspoon vanilla extract
8 thin lemon slices

Mix all-purpose flour, cake flour, 1 tablespoon sugar and $^1/_2$ teaspoon salt in food processor. Cut in 6 tablespoons butter and shortening, pulsing until crumbly. Add ice water. Process until moist clumps form, adding additional water by teaspoonfuls if needed.

Gather dough into ball; flatten into disk. Chill, wrapped in plastic wrap, for 1 hour to 2 days. Let dough soften slightly at room temperature before rolling.

Roll into 12-inch circle on lightly floured surface. Fit into buttered 9-inch glass pie plate. Trim edge, leaving $^1/_2$-inch overhang. Crimp overhang decoratively. Freeze for 15 minutes.

Line pastry with foil; fill with dried beans or pie weights. Bake at 350 degrees for 20 minutes or until crust is set and edge is pale golden brown. Remove beans and foil. Cool completely.

Beat eggs, egg yolks and $^1/_4$ teaspoon salt in large mixer bowl until blended. Add $1^1/_4$ cups sugar. Beat for 1 minute or until thick and fluffy. Beat in coconut, $^1/_4$ cup whipping cream, lemon juice, 2 tablespoons butter, lemon peel, $1^1/_2$ teaspoons vanilla and almond extract.

Pour into crust. Bake at 350 degrees for 40 minutes or until filling is golden brown and set. Cool in pie plate on wire rack. Refrigerate, covered, for 3 hours or until thoroughly chilled. May be prepared 1 day ahead.

Beat $^3/_4$ cup whipping cream, confectioners' sugar and $^3/_4$ teaspoon vanilla in large mixer bowl until stiff peaks form. Pipe around border of pie. Top with lemon slices.

Yield: 8 servings

DESSERTS

Fool's Toffee

1 cup butter
1 cup packed dark brown sugar
35 saltines
2 cups chocolate chips
$^1/_2$ cup pecan or walnut pieces

Line 10x15-inch jelly roll pan with foil. Butter lightly. Combine butter and brown sugar in small saucepan. Bring to a boil over medium heat. Boil for 4 minutes.

Arrange crackers close together in single layer in prepared pan. Spread butter mixture evenly over crackers. Bake at 375 degrees for 5 minutes.

Sprinkle with chocolate chips. Let soften and spread evenly. Sprinkle with pecans.

Chill until cool. Break into pieces. Store in airtight container in refrigerator for up to 2 weeks.

Yield: 15 servings

Heavenly Hard Sauce

$^1/_2$ cup unsalted butter, softened
$^1/_2$ cup confectioners' sugar
$^1/_2$ teaspoon vanilla extract or
fruit-flavored liqueur

Beat butter in mixing bowl until light and fluffy. Add confectioners' sugar gradually, whipping well after each addition. Stir in vanilla.

Chill for 1 hour. Serve with plum pudding.

Yield: $^3/_4$ cup

DESSERTS

Hot Fudge Sauce

2 ounces unsweetened chocolate
1 tablespoon butter
$^1/_3$ cup boiling water
$^1/_8$ teaspoon salt
1 cup sugar
2 tablespoons corn syrup
1 teaspoon vanilla extract, or 2 teaspoons rum

Melt chocolate and butter in double boiler over simmering water. Add boiling water, salt, sugar and corn syrup and mix gently. Bring to a rapid boil without stirring. Boil for 8 minutes.
Stir in vanilla just before serving.

Yield: $^3/_4$ to 1 cup

Raisinberry Sauce

$2^1/_2$ cups golden raisins
2 cups freshly squeezed orange juice
1 cup water
$^1/_4$ cup freshly squeezed lemon juice
1 cup sugar
3 cups cranberries
1 tablespoon grated orange peel

Combine raisins, orange juice, water, lemon juice and sugar in saucepan. Bring to a boil, stirring until sugar dissolves; reduce heat. Simmer for 10 minutes, stirring occasionally.
Add cranberries and orange peel. Boil for 5 minutes or until cranberries begin to pop. Let cool.

Yield: $4^1/_2$ cups

DESSERTS

Contributors List

Buster Crab Seafood
Cafe Bernard
Harry Caray's
  Restaurant
Erwin—An American
  Cafe & Bar
Frontera Grill
Hotel Ritz
Michael Jordan's
  Restaurant
Marshall Field's
Lee Abbott
Abby Ackerman
Chef Abraham
  Aguirre
Maggie Alexander
Bethy Apley
Susan Artman
Cheryl Bailey
Anne Q. Barr
Polly Bauer
Linda Beck
Cindy Berry
Nina Bliese
Sandy Boettcher
Linda W. Bricker
Jack Brickhouse
Julie Pfeiffer Brooks
Jamie Lynn Burd
Stephanie Grahn
  Burnsed
Marianne Cahill
Rachel Landen
  Carlson
Andrea Castione
Mrs. Robert Cave
Nancy Deal Chandler
Lisa Churchville
Kerstin Hruska Clark
Julie Coker
Mary Cooper
Kim Blazek Dahlborn
Mayor and Mrs. Daley

Leslie Delany
Abbie Deneen
Donnelle DePrey
Melinda DiPerna
Catherine M.
  Dohnalek
Governor and
  Mrs. Jim Edgar
Nancy Ervin
Grace Everett
Natalie Macdonald
  Ferry
Patricia L. Fraser
Bonita Friedland
Barbara Gartner
LuAnn Gavula
Nancy Gee
Carol Genis
Leonora Gillette
Liz Goebel
Sue-Gray Goller
Kimberlea D.
  Goodman
Judith C. Goodwin
Polly Grafton
Lisa Gray
Dianne Gregg
Will R. Gregg III
Kim Marie Gryka
Bryant Gumbel
Elaine Harris
Kim Hartman
Heidi Helgens
Sharon Hellman
Mary J. Hill
Julie Hughes
Cynthia Humphry
Elizabeth Imus
Ginny Fuller Istnick
Jayne Johnson
Betsy Johnston
Kathy Johnston
Chef Michael Kalanty

Ann Vismara Kay
Debra Kempf-Stolbof
Lynne Kerger
Millie Kerger
Nancy Gillespy
  Kimberly
Ann Kingstrom
Shannon Kinsella
Sharon R. Knitter
Terry C. Kreissl
Vicky S. Kujawa
Clara Van Derzee
  Lang
Nora Larkin
Rita Lashmet
Carolyn Legor
Dorothy Lenzie
Miriam Lifsics
Jeanne Long
Cathy McInerney
  Lynch
Nedra Lynest
Ann MacDiarmid
Mary MacDiarmid
Nellie MacDiarmid
Nicole Mack
Sarah Magner
Aimee Maher
Kathy Malherbe
Kathryn Bader
  Mangel
Deborah Marcusson
Cathy Mataloni
Helen McCabe
Ellen McCarthy
Gail Quigley McCarthy
Lynne McCoy
Maureen McMeel
Cindy Memmen
Tom Memmen
Kristin A. Merrigan
Sandra Michelau
Lori Midson

Alyson Montgomery
Laura Moran
Janet Morano
Margaret Mordy
Laurie Munick
Dee Murray
Mary Neary
Clara Nelson
Nena Nesset
Ruby Niessen
Annette Nikolich
Cynthia Nottoli
Peggy Nuccio
Ric Nuccio
Ruby Nussiw
Nan Nygaard
Penny Obenshain
Hermanda de Roos
  O'Connor
Mimi Ogden
Diane Okel
Kitty Knox Oldham
Penny Clarke Ose
Mrs. Tom Parsons
Alice Peterson
Wilma Pfeiffer
Elizabeth Baldwin
  Phillips
Cathryn Ploger
Sharon Pohl
Anita "Sam" Pollack
Oren T. Pollack
Suzanne S. Pollock
Tammy J. Pretasky
Leta Quigley
Amy Rardin
Cindie Remm
Karen Restum
Bernice Retzke
Linda Reynolds
Marilyn Reynolds
Ann Marie Rigali
Molly Riley

Julie Ann Rogers
Mary Rownd
Camille Kearns
  Rudy
Pamela Russell
Betts Ryan
Lynda Santos
Deena Schencker
Deborah Schmidt
Rose Schumacher
Jan Sennott
Janet Smart
Sara Smith
Tobie F. Smith
Sheridan Snell
Sally Soule
Liz Stiffel
Mary Jane Jennings
  Stutz
Dr. Toy Suddeth
Beverly J. Suhrheinrich
Diana Sweemer
Courtney A.
  Thompson
Suzy Thompson
Jean Tindall
Ali Tucker
Elonda Ware
Carol Janson Welles
Heather Wennink
Mimi Peters Westin
Pamela White
Marijke Woodruff
Barbara Ann Wright
Susan Yatman
Meredith Zelewsky

Special Thanks to the
following chefs:
Rick Bayless
Robert Childers
Laurence Roney

Index

INDEX

237

INDEX

Neighborhood Photography:

©Lee Balterman 1992/FPG International, 137; ©Zbigniew Bzdak, 25, 73, 124, 144, 166; Churchill & Klehr, 115; Brent Jones, 36, 78; ©Cathy Melloan/Tony Stone Images, 10; ©Paul Merideth/Tony Stone Images, 219; ©Peter Pearson/Tony Stone Images, 102; ©Marc Pokempner/ Tony Stone Images, 177; Ron Schramm Photography, 7, 58, 157, 184, 202; ©Mark Segal/Tony Stone Images, 3

INDEX